PRAISE FOR
DON'T BURP IN THE BOARDROOM

"Don't get caught unprepared. Knowing how to conduct yourself with civility and tact is an incredible advantage in today's workforce. *Don't Burp in the Boardroom* is a must-read for college grads, as well as the long-time employee!"

—Frank Shankwitz, Retired Arizona Department of Public Safety Detective and Co-Founder of the Make-A-Wish Foundation

"Rosalinda Randall here-in provides an impressive compendium of straight-forward, common sense nuggets of wisdom for handling life's often awkward and/or unexpected dilemmas—dilemmas many of us often find we are unprepared to deal with.

"This is a very easy, charismatic, and informative read laced with lightheartedness. Anyone who values being better prepared for life and the unexpected will surely benefit from the contents of these pages."

—Matt Helm, Owner of Matt Helm Entertainment
(Dean Martin/Sean Connery Impersonator)

"Saying what you mean without ⬛⬛⬛⬛⬛⬛⬛ ᵈᵃᵗion of good relationships and successfu⬛ ⬛⬛⬛⬛⬛⬛ of a college and a former NFL pla⬛ ⬛⬛⬛⬛ act with others has a direct im⬛ ⬛⬛⬛⬛ success. *Don't Burp in the Boardroom* ⬛⬛ etiquette, with real-life situations and solutions that are ⬛⬛ ⬛⬛⬛

in the locker room and classroom as they are in a boardroom. Every professional team, no matter how large or small, will benefit from Rosalinda's advice!"

—Ted Petersen, Director of Athletics and Physical Education, former offensive lineman for Pittsburgh Steelers (1977–1983, 1987), Cleveland Browns (1984), Indianapolis Colts (1984)

"*Don't Burp in the Boardroom* is the must-read manual of the century! It basically gives a less-skilled person the fundamentals of etiquette and the basic knowledge to succeed in the workplace. It covers everything from how to use a napkin to social media tips. I personally discovered things I could improve on. To be frank there are not very many things I would recommend but *Don't Burp in the Boardroom* takes a fascinating look at daily etiquette; it is on my short list of recommended books."

—Stanley Roberts, Creator and Producer of award-winning "People Behaving Badly" KRON 4 TV San Francisco

"*Don't Burp In The Boardroom* by etiquette expert Rosalinda Randall is a humorous but all-too-real look at the office etiquette issues facing the modern professional of almost any stripe today. Randall doesn't just give advice on the superficial—how to dress, or what to order at a business lunch etc., although those are covered as well—but takes a hard look at many of the questions facing fresh job-seekers or even long-time employees, viewing situations from different perspectives. She then proceeds to break those challenges down into manageable components and presents various solutions for different outcomes, in a rather refreshing approach.

"Whether you're new to the workforce or a seasoned office veteran, the crucial insight Randall provides in the book may mean the difference between getting that job or promotion, or losing the opportunity altogether. *Don't Burp in the Boardroom* may also prove invaluable to those who lead or manage people—after all, office etiquette is appreciated at every level!"

—Daniel Goh, Editor of YoungUpstarts.com

"Whether you are an entrepreneur climbing the ladder or patrolling the beat, the way you conduct yourself matters. If you want to make a great impression, the first day and every day, Rosalinda offers applicable, real-life solutions to real-life dilemmas for employees in today's competitive workplace. Don't apply for another job or deal with that hard-to-live-with coworker until you've read *Don't Burp in the Boardroom*."

—Jamie Monozon, CEO San Bruno Chamber of Commerce

"*Don't Burp in the Boardroom* is a no-nonsense guide for young graduates to navigate the etiquette hallways of the workplace. Rosalinda Oropeza Randall is an expert in her field and delivers etiquette advice in a down-to-earth manner. Her advice is full of anecdotal stories and examples that clearly illustrate the value of her knowledge. This book is a must-have for anyone looking to be successful at work."

—Candice Nance, International Business Professor, Cañada College

DON'T

BURP

IN THE

BOARD

ROOM

Rosalinda Oropeza Randall

Published by Familius LLC, www.familius.com

Familius books are available at special discounts for bulk purchases for sales promotions, family or corporate use. Special editions, including personalized covers, excerpts of existing books, or books with corporate logos, can be created in large quantities for special needs. For more information, contact Premium Sales at 559-876-2170 or email specialmarkets@familius.com

Library of Congress Catalog-in-Publication Data

2014948926

pISBN 978-1-939629-35-7
eISBN 978-1-939629-49-4

Printed in the United States of America

Edited by Brooke Jorden
Cover design by David Miles
Book design by David Miles and Maggie Wickes
Illustrations by Tiffany Sheely

10 9 8 7 6 5 4 3 2 1

First Edition

For my parents, Dirce and Enrique Oropeza.
Con mucho cariño les dedico este libro.

CONTENTS

ACKNOWLEDGMENTS

An enormous thank you to Familius Publishing for making it possible for me to publish this book. I am especially grateful to Christopher Robbins and David Miles for their interest even after I said, "It's about etiquette." Thank you for having faith in me and in what I had to say.

My editors, Brooke Jorden and Maggie Wickes, who encouraged me to express myself and to stay true to my message. I appreciate your calm guidance throughout the process and for shedding light when I needed things spelled out. Thank you.

A special recognition and heartfelt gratitude to Jacqueline Whitmore, founder of The Protocol School of Palm Beach, for your generous counsel, for encouraging me to write the book, and for being the inspiration for the title of this book. You are a true professional. Thank you, Jacqueline.

A special thank you to Maria Goodavage, *New York Times* best-selling author of *Soldier Dogs*. Your insight and sage perspective was timely. You proved that two heads are better than one to spark ideas.

And for your creativity and vision, my illustrator, Tiffany Sheely, you always seemed to "get me" and knew exactly what I wanted. Thank you.

Patti McKenna, thank you for encouraging me to make the most of this experience. I am grateful to you for your generous spirit, wisdom, knowledge, and honest advice throughout these past few months.

To my colleagues and experts; you so readily contributed by providing your professional services, serving as a source, and sharing your insight and wisdom: Alina Steinberg Baugh, Rachel Capil, Suzi Desmond, Monique Hunter, Kristina Lopez, Arlene Miller, Diane Paisley, Robert G. Pimm, and Constance Kobylarz Wilde. I value our association and am grateful to you for your assistance. And to many others who have encouraged me—too many to mention—thank you.

To the few who intimately saw me through this book: My cousin, Laura Ligia Dodie. Thanks for cray-cray conversations and the laughs that went with it. My friend, Phyllis Garland who listened to my random silliness and just laughed along. My sister and brother, Rebeca and Gilberto Oropeza who always checked in on me and filled me on the family happenings during my sequester. And my sister-in-law Karen McGovern who cheerfully hosted the holiday gatherings so that I could continue writing and just show up. Thank you.

To my mother-in-law, Effie Randall, thank you for your prayers and encouraging words. And my mom and dad, Enrique and Dirce Oropeza for bringing me up right and for being my inspiration.

My children, Ryan, Kelly, Alexander, and Jonnalyn. In spite of all the time it took me away from you, you encouraged me and even advised me. Thank you for being a part of this. It is a privilege to be your mom. (The best job that I ever had!)

My husband, Christopher, your support and reassurance allowed me to become an author. Never saying anything when you ate dinners alone, after cooking it too. You are my dream husband. Thank you so much for encouraging me and not saying anything when I typed through the night—night after night, after night—or about the uniform of the day, pajamas, day after day after day. I love you.

A *joie de vivre* mention to French music (the old stuff), for inspiring me while I wrote.

And to the Big Guy in the Sky, thank you.

I beg forgiveness of anyone whose name I may have failed to mention.

AUTHOR'S NOTE

Dear reader: Books are a dime a dozen, and everybody's got an opinion. So, on the off chance that this book is helpful or even simply amuses you, thank you. You've made it worthwhile.

The purpose of this book is to inspire more courteous communication and to encourage a more good-natured and gracious outlook and temperament when handling life's dilemmas. How? By allowing courtesy, consideration, tact, respect, humility and humor to be your guide.

Plainly speaking: A person who exemplifies these traits typically does not create dilemmas; they usually help resolve them.

I am by nature fiery, so I'm sure that I've been guilty of one or two faux pas that I write about in this book. Because of the strong foundation my parents instilled in me, I was able to hold back (most of the time) and reconsider my words and actions.

FOREWORD

You're in line at the supermarket and you're just about to put your groceries onto the checkout counter. You notice the man behind you has only two items. What do you do? Do you ignore him? Do you point him towards the express lane? Or do you invite him to go in front of you?

The truth is, you define who you are every day by the choices you make and the way you treat others. You are not what you eat; you are what you think.

Rosalinda Randall gets it. She knows that etiquette is an attitude—that is, a system of beliefs that causes us to treat others a certain way. She knows that etiquette has evolved over time. Etiquette is situational.

In today's complex society, it's more important than ever to hone your "situational awareness." That is, pay attention to your environment, relationships, and circumstances so you can proactively influence the situation with tact, diplomacy, and grace.

In this book, you'll discover that etiquette is a set of unwritten rules that apply to social situations, professional workplaces, and relationships. It is one of the many keys to help you progress in your career and in life. When you treat others the way they would like to be treated, you stand out from the crowd and get rewarded and recognized.

But it's simpler than that. When you perform small acts

of kindness—sending a card, giving a compliment, or doing someone a favor—it costs little to nothing and leaves a lasting impression. The choices you make and the words you say can also profoundly impact others on a larger scale.

In the 1946 classic, *It's a Wonderful Life*, George (played by James Stewart) is given the rare opportunity to see how the world would look if he never existed. He realizes that the lives he has touched goes far beyond the boundaries of his small community of Bedford Falls. Your influence in the world is like a rock thrown in a pond. The rock will quickly disappear but the ripples left behind go on and on.

Rosalinda and I met nearly five years ago when she called and asked to join my etiquette mastermind group, The Consultants Connection. As our friendship grew, I realized that she was no ordinary etiquette expert. She was something more.

She is witty, has a keen sense of humor, and has a caring heart. She knows how to interact with people from all walks of life. Like me, she didn't grow up attending tea parties or cotillions. Our working-class parents instilled in us important values and good manners. Rosalinda's background makes her real and relatable.

You're probably reading this book because you want to acquire more confidence. Perhaps you're looking for advice in these pages that will strengthen your resolve, boost your self-esteem, reduce your anxieties and fears, and help you grow personally and professionally. If so, keep reading. Rosalinda is your expert.

You'll find the information in this book to be direct, easy to understand, and effective. Yes, these tips really do work. If you follow Rosalinda's advice, you'll not only reap the rewards, you'll attract more joy and contentment in your life.

— Jacqueline Whitmore, founder of The Protocol School of Palm Beach and author of *Poised for Success: Mastering the Four Qualities That Distinguish Outstanding Professionals*

INTRODUCTION

Old-School Workplace Advice (and a little bit about me)

Advice from my mother-in-law, Effie Randall: "The three best things people can do for each other are to be clean, to keep yourself healthy, and to be happy."

Workplace advice from my dad, Enrique Oropeza: "To get ahead, work hard, work harder, do more than you are asked or expected to do, and do it with pride, no matter what the job is."

My mom, Dirce, would add, "If you are a sweeper, be the best sweeper. If you can't do that job well, why would they give you a promotion?"

How's that for instilling work ethic?

So, when things were slow in the office, I would dust, fill the copy machine, disinfect stuff, straighten things up—whatever it took to keep busy. And why not? It had to be done anyway. Just because it wasn't listed in my job description didn't mean I couldn't do it. Don't you want a clean work environment? You might be thinking, *That's what the janitor gets paid to do.* Well, either dusting isn't in his job description, or he isn't very thorough.

> "Tell the truth, work hard, and come to dinner on time." -Gerald R. Ford, 38th President of the United States

ABOUT THE BOOK

Have you stayed at an unpleasant job longer than you wanted to because you liked your coworkers? Did the camaraderie get you through the day? If so, you might agree that how you behave and/or your attitude play a huge role in the lives of those around you—especially in the workplace.

Since we've all got to go to work at some point, why not make it a more pleasant place to be? (I know that's slightly corny, but I bet you agree.)

This book is written in a truly modern, thoroughly practical manner with an unvarnished approach, sprinkled with cheeky humor. I've gone beyond the fluffy stuff, addressing today's workplace culture and all of its ever-changing attitudes—the good, the bad, and the uncommonly common.

Instead of immovable rules, I offer options, because there is always more than one way to handle a dilemma. Besides, no one likes to be told what to do! Every situation and personality requires consideration before you jump and attack, or get offended.

My point for offering options is to underline that you can *say what you mean without being mean*, while accenting the think-before-you-react approach. My options are not for everyone, nor are they your only options. Look at it as a guidebook.

I stand by and believe that the desire for etiquette and good manners is there. However, sometimes it is devalued or kicked to the curb as passé at the expense of being comfortable, casual, free-thinking, friendly, and "not-corporate."

Etiquette is an attitude. Whether you are in a three-piece power suit, have an apron wrapped around your waist, or wear work boots and jeans, you have a choice to be nasty or nice. Being nice cannot be imposed by any rules or laws.

In the end, it is your professional reputation you're building or destroying.

P.S. Please note that a sense of humor is required while reading this book. I have no doubt that someone will find something I've said offensive, indelicate, or downright wrong! If it's you, I sincerely apologize. It is not my intent to insult anyone. If something offends you, my recommendation to you is to skip to the next part. Thank you.

Here's another reason to read this book and keep it by your side:
"Always read something that will make you look good if you die in the middle of it."–P.J. O'Rourke, American political satirist, journalist, writer and author

---

DON'T BURP IN THE BOARDROOM

Prominently featuring "the burp" in the title of a book might seem odd, but I believe the diminishment of a professional atmosphere begins with something as insignificant and natural as the burp.

As a society, we determine what is and is not acceptable behavior. Burping, yelling, interrupting, responding rudely, being late, etc., are still considered unprofessional. People do it, but we don't like it.

A burp is necessary, but gross—just like picking the gook from the corner of your eyes, flicking the outer-edge of your nose, rubbing your toes, scratching your body parts, and so on. Our society has deemed these as distasteful acts to do in public.

> Next time you attend a meeting, be aware of the itching and scratching and picking and burping that goes on. But be warned! Once you become aware of it, you won't be able to focus on the speaker.

While it may be acceptable in front of your family and friends, the boardroom isn't usually filled with your family and friends; therefore, a different set of rules apply. And that is *professionalism*. Unfortunately, the extreme informality we practice at home can become habit.

> "To change a habit, make a conscious decision, then act out the new behavior." —Maxwell Maltz, American cosmetic surgeon and image consultant

Is burping in the boardroom a career-killing deed? No. But it can give the boss cause to deduce that:

- you'll "let your hair down" when you think no one is looking.
- you don't have the sense or polish to determine what is considered appropriate behavior.
- you let out a self-satisfying burp today . . . what's next—breaking wind?

Naturally, slips from either end happen no matter how much you try to hold them in. Those are quite forgivable. Simply mutter, "Pardon me," and move on.

"Enjoy your lunch, Tess?"

KEY POINTS:

- Be the one to bring back a little old-school tradition.
- If something needs to be done, just do it.
- Don't bring your "home" habits to work.
- Be clean, be efficient, and be kind—in short, be professional.

CHAPTER 1

FIRST IMPRESSIONS

Here comes a "preachy" moment. However you choose to live your life, handle dilemmas, dress, or behave is totally up to you. But—and it's a big but—as with everything, there are reactions and consequences, like it or not. Okay, I'm done.

Do you want to dress in your comfortable, worn-in jeans, your favorite flip-flops that have trekked across the world with you, or a peasant skirt with a darling tank top to a job interview? Fine, but you've arrived with a strike or two against you. "That sucks," you say? Perhaps, but that's just the way it is. Rhetorical question: what's your goal and what are you trying to prove or accomplish?

There are time-honored traditions that remain the standard in the workplace, no matter how much you try to ignore or invalidate them from everyday life. They remain because most people like them—there's a purpose.

Don't you react to what you see? Let's say you are introduced to a guy wearing a cuffed beanie, blue vintage shoes, skinny jeans, and a bold-striped hoodie. (Cute and trendy, right? Well, it was at the time this book was written.) Would you:

A   Extend your right hand to shake: "Hello, I'm Mateo Randall. How do you do?"

B   Extend your right hand to shake: "Hey, what's up? I'm Mateo."

What if the same person is wearing slacks, a dress shirt, a casual sport coat, and dress shoes? Would you introduce yourself in the same way? Come on, tell the truth.

It's not a bad thing. I'm just pointing out that we use our instincts (which can be wrong) to react and respond.

How do you want to be *perceived*? Is making a fashion statement more important than making the right impression? You decide, and go for it.

The same applies to our demeanor. For example, is a small, privately-owned business more likely to accept a more relaxed attitude? What if it's a law office, cosmetic surgeon, therapist, or accounting service?

Certain industries require a more professional and even conservative look and demeanor.

As a first impression, which scenario would create confidence and display professionalism and expertise in your mind?

A As you walk into the office, the receptionist is chewing gum, loudly responding to the caller who is on the telephone canceling an appointment, and while rolling her eyes she is waving her hand to the person standing behind you to go in.

B As you walk into the office, the receptionist, even though on the telephone, looks up at you and smiles as she gives the "I'll-be-right-with-you" nod. She is speaking in a confidential voice to the caller, asking the caller if he can hold for just a moment. After placing the caller on hold, she says to the person seated behind you, "Excuse me, Mr. Oropeza, they are ready for you now."

Hmm. See how a subtle gesture can set the mood? That is why I focus on the small stuff, like responding "yes" instead of "yeah," "no" instead of "uh-uh," avoiding openly burping in the boardroom, and dressing professionally.

....

THE HANDSHAKE

Limpy = Wimpy, Solid = Savvy

Did you know that, in some cases, business decisions are made based on the handshake? Crazy, right? I've had women tell me that if a man shakes her hand in a delicate manner, it's over before it begins. A little harsh, maybe, but it illustrates my point.

To exude confidence and competence, like anything else, it takes practice. If you aren't sure whether your handshake is limpy or solid, ask a trusted friend.

In the United States, and specifically in the workplace, the handshake is gender neutral and, in most cases, can be initiated by either sex.

A business handshake should be brief. (At around six to seven seconds, we are ready to release the grip.) You don't want to pump your client's hand to the point where both your palms begin to perspire and become stuck together. And you certainly do not want to go to an extreme by overdoing the firm grip. It isn't a bodybuilding competition, and it can be viewed just as negatively as the limpy shake.

When is it customary to shake hands?

- When you introduce yourself.
- As a greeting when you enter an office and again upon exiting.
- To congratulate someone (even when you are the loser).
- Instead of a hug.
- To make a promise or seal a deal (a little old-school).
- When you thank someone.

You might not shake hands when:

- your hands are full (box of bagels, coffee).
- you are eating. (You don't want their germs on your hands; you can bet they don't want sticky sauce on theirs.)

- you are contagious. (This may be awkward if they just sneezed into their hand and then extended it to shake—go ahead and shake it anyway.)
- your hands are dirty (taco sauce or toner from the copy machine).
- there is a disability involved. (It's not always obvious; don't ask.)
- you saw them only moments ago. (For coworkers you see on a daily basis, a simple "good morning" will do.)
- there is a religious or personal reason.
- you go in for a big hug instead. (Please don't do this; most people are uncomfortable with this in a business setting.)

Handshaking "Habitudes"

What is your handshake habitude? What will my experience be when I shake hands with you? Will I stay or will I go?

Will it be awkward? Unfriendly? Sticky? Uncomfortably drawn-out? Quick and abrupt? What perception of you will I take away with me?

Note for the ladies: Don't get all crazy and revolutionary on a man if he shakes your hand in a delicate manner. In most cases, his intentions are noble. He is not trying to "put you in your place," make a pass at you, or make you feel inferior to him.

If there is a discreet way of slipping your hand into his to firmly shake, fine; if not, forget about it and get to know him.

Hesitant and delicate. Appropriate only if you are afraid of the opposite sex, you are just about to waltz, or they smell. How will you hear what they are saying?

Top: Incorrect. Too genteel. Bottom: Firm and fully engaged. Fingers grip the meaty part.

Familiar greeting. Placing your hand on someone's elbow or shoulder is appropriate when you haven't seen each other in a while, when greeting an out-of-town coworker/client that you've known for a while, after a promotion, congratulating, or offering your condolences. It can be considered a "business hug." Keep some distance.

A bit delicate. She won't break, Mister. He's making no effort in extending his arm. And stopped short of a firm grip. Looks a little like a junior high dance.

That is how you'll really know what he thinks.

If you lack confidence in shaking hands, practice, practice, practice, and master it.

Did you know?

In some cultures, it is considered rude to put out your left hand. That is the hand used primarily for hygiene duty.

From the Audience:

Q: My hands tend to get sweaty. I am really self-conscious when I attend business functions where handshaking is non-stop. What do you recommend? —Lloyd

A: Dear Lloyd,

This is not an uncommon problem. One option is to apply deodorant to your hands. Be aware that some deodorants are sticky and will leave people's hands smelling like fresh mountain air. If that doesn't appeal to you, consider applying a sprinkle of talcum powder or an alcohol-based hand sanitizer to dry up the skin. You can also regularly wash your hands in cold water, giving them a chance to cool off.

A quick solution is a smooth-move wipe of your hand on the side of your thigh as you lift it to shake hands. Another option is to hold a napkin in your hand to absorb the moisture.

Typically, I advise people to hold their beverage in their left hand, leaving the right hand dry and at room temperature. However, in this case, bending the rule can help you. As you transfer the cold beverage to your left hand, your right hand will be damp and cool. Make an attempt to dry it on a napkin or your thigh. Smile, and say something like, "Please forgive the frosty hand." They'll attribute the damp handshake to your beverage.

5 Keys to the Perfect Handshake:

- Stand (unless you are ill, have a broken leg, or you're holding a baby in your lap—common sense, people)
- Smile (even if you don't feel like it, or aren't glad to see the person)
- Firm Grip (How to gauge? Think equal to holding a full glass of water.)
- Right Hand (even if you are left-handed or the person extends their left hand, which could feel klutzy—always use your right hand)
- Eye Contact (Don't look beyond them to see if someone more exciting enters the room. That is probably one of the rudest things you can do to a person—focus; it's only a few seconds!)

From the Audience:

Q: I extended my hand to shake, but the woman did not extend hers in return. I felt pretty stupid. I think she realized it because she began talking about the event. What should I have done?—John

A: Dear John,

People do not extend their hand for various reasons like religious restrictions, mysophobia (germ OCD), bad manicure, or extreme shyness. Even though your facial expression may have given you away, you should have gone on as though she had shaken your hand. By the way, never ask why.

> Don't speak about your oozing cold sore; "How are you?" is a greeting, and is not meant to be a question.

Q: I was approached by a person who, only moments before, I observed licking their fingers. I made up an excuse so that I would not have to touch their hand. Was I correct in doing so? —Antoine

A: Dear Antoine,

No one blames you—but no. Never turn down a handshake unless you have a religious restriction, just licked your own fingers, or have a broken finger. After the sticky handshake and chit chat, you could have discreetly escaped to the restroom to wash your hands. If you stop to think about where someone's fingers have been, you probably wouldn't shake hands with anyone unless you were wearing protective rubber gloves.

As for your idea of giving some excuse like, "Forgive me, but I'm fighting a cold . . . " they could come back with, "Why are you here spreading your germs?" You will look and feel like a chump. And, if "sticky fingers" catches you shaking hands with someone else, uh, awkward!

....

INTRODUCING
YOURSELF

Start with some sort of greeting: "Good morning (afternoon, evening)" or "Hello" ("Hi" is not bad, but a bit casual in a workplace, especially at an interview or when you first meet someone; why not go upscale?)

By the way, a "How do you do?" (although a bit 1940s) really is the best choice. (Don't get melodramatic or add a British accent when you say it, and don't use the downright-neighborly "How d'ya do?")

"It's a pleasure to meet you" and "It's nice to meet you" are perfectly fine to use, but if you think about it, how do you know whether they are a "pleasure" or "nice" to meet? If you know of them or heard fabulous things about them, then you might consider using those phrases. Please keep in mind that, whatever you say, it's all in the tone.

The Hugger

Hugging in the workplace should probably not happen very often. For one, it can be misconstrued—by the recipient or an onlooker. If the hugging couple is of different genders, there is an added complication.

When is hugging acceptable? Anytime you want, really. However, not everyone feels the same. That is why I recommend refraining from this type of greeting, with a few possible exceptions:

- The hugger is from another country where a whole-hearted embrace is the norm. (Not your thing? Oh well, sometimes it just happens.)

- Someone you've known only through online communication is in town, and you meet; a brief hug could ensue.

- A colleague announced that they are having a baby, are leaving the company, are receiving a promotion, won the lottery, are visiting from another location, or lost a loved one.

How to Avoid a Hugger:

- Be ready! As the hugger approaches, turn your body slightly to the left and extend your right hand. This will prompt the hugger to do the same, simultaneously putting space between you.

- If the hugger has already encroached, place your left hand, open palm, against their upper right shoulder while extending your right hand to shake. (It is imperative that your palm rest on their upper shoulder, especially if the hugger is a female—any lower . . . well, you can imagine.)

- Be honest with them. In a cordial tone, smile and say, "Ryan, if you don't mind, I'd prefer to shake hands." Immediately go on with the conversation.

Please Don't Call Me That!

Me: Hello, I'm Rosalinda Randall. How do you do?

Guest: Hello, Rosa. I'm Pablo Pushypants. How's it going?

Me: How do you do, Pablo. (In my head: *Um, not well. I hate to be called Rosa!* But I complete the greeting and say nothing more.)

Do you resort to abbreviating names because:

- you are too lazy to say it?
- it's too difficult to remember? (Most people are happy to repeat it.)
- you don't like my name?
- you hope it will break down walls and we'll become BFFs in a minute?
- it's your thing?
- it's cultural? (Okay, that I believe. In the Hispanic culture, it is quite common to modify names and/or add a little endearing word ending. Rosalinda might be Rosi or Rosita; Teresa might be Teresita or Tere; Francisco, Pancho; Enrique, Quique. This is not necessarily appropriate in a business setting, but it can happen in a social setting.)

Rosalinda Gets Personal:

I'm not a fan when someone automatically abbreviates my name. "Oh, it's too long. Don't you have a shorter version?" Uh, lady, by the time you ask me that question, you could have said my name! My philosophy on this is that if I will be seeing you again, I'll correct you, but if I won't, I'll let it go. Recently, a service provider came to my home. He called me Rosie. I don't expect my appliance to break down again anytime soon, so I let it go.

I Didn't Get Your Name

I'm Gumersinda Prewitt. How do you do? (Gumer-wha'?)

What do you do when you don't understand or hear the person's name? Simple.

"I'm sorry, would you please repeat your name?" Or "I will do my best to learn your name. Until then, I hope you don't mind if I ask you to repeat it." Or any variation of these.

Note to people with unique names: please say your name slowly and speak clearly. (Eye contact helps.) Thank you.

> Don't use your cutesy nickname at work. An abbreviated version of your name is fine. Refer to a person by the name they give you! In addition, people who have unusual or lengthy names are used to repeating them; just ask.

INTERVIEWS

Mr. Zippy-Pants' Interview Ends Before It Begins.

It begins in the parking lot. Well, actually, it begins the moment you step out of your home. I refer to making a good impression.

Picture it: You're running late, and of course every bad driver is on the road that day. Your car horn has never received so much attention; you're zipping in and out of the fast lane trying to get to your interview on time. You've cut a couple of cars off. Oh well, they should have been in the slow lane anyway. And just to let everyone know how agitated they're making you feel today, up goes your finger: the universal gesture of displeasure.

You zip into the parking lot, cutting off the pedestrian, but you made it—on time!

You open the door so quickly it bumps the car next to you . . . whatever.

You adjust your undies.

You are on your cell phone blasting your mom for not waking you up after your snooze alarm went off. (Not her job—just sayin'.)

You stick your finger up your nose, making sure nothing's up there. And you're ready.

As you walk toward the entrance and wait by the elevator, two other people approach. When you've reached your floor, one of them exits with you; you get a strange vibe.

As you enter the conference room (or interviewer's office), you are greeted with a "In a rush this morning, Mr. Zippy-Pants?" In your head, you wonder whether he was the one whose car you bumped your door against, the one you almost ran over in the parking lot, the one who overheard the disagreeable conversation you were having with your mom, or the lucky recipient of your highway finger gesture. (Does it really matter? All bad.)

What can you do or say? Nothing.

You might stand a chance if the person has an unconventional sense of humor, they handle life in the same way as you and think nothing of it, or they give you the benefit of the doubt and see how you conduct yourself in the interview.

If not, you may have blown the interview before it even started.

> Avoid "And your name was?" (It still is . . .)

Interviewing Basics to Consider

Smile. Walk in with some energy. (Remember, you're supposed to be interested and eager to get this job—show it.)

Dress up. (If your three-year-old stained khakis are your best, what's to come?)

Leave the cell phone off and the double-pump latte in the car. (Walking in with stuff—just don't.)

Sit up straight. (A relaxed position can be construed as arrogant.)

Don't ever be rude to the receptionist/administrative professional. (They have input, and it's just not nice.)

Bring extra copies of your résumé, as well as a pen and notepad. (This shows that you think ahead and are prepared.)

Never, *ever* start by inquiring about pay, benefits, vacation time, lunchroom perks, or how big your office may be. (Lose the "what's-in-it-for-me" attitude.)

Do not bad-mouth previous employers, bosses, or co-workers. (That only shows your lack of discretion and that you play the blame game.)

Stop and listen.

Don't use foul language or terms like, "Dude," "bro," "hey," or "I'm good to go."

Don't lie or exaggerate about your skills. (Not only is this embarrassing when you get caught, but you will certainly not get the job.)

Disclose your criminal background, but use discretion. You may want to wait until the end of the interview (once they've had a chance to "like" you). Some people might say this is sneaky and this information should be disclosed immediately. Again, that's a personal decision. If it directly affects your ability to do the job, of course you should divulge this information right away (e.g., revoked driver's license and the job requires travelling). Otherwise, use your best judgment.

Shake hands, say "Thank you," and be sure to get their name (so that you can send a thank-you note).

The Waiting Area

Which man looks ready to stand up and introduce himself in this picture?

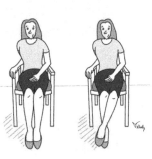

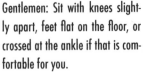

Gentlemen: Sit with knees slightly apart, feet flat on the floor, or crossed at the ankle if that is comfortable for you.

Ladies: Sit with knees together, feet flat on the floor or crossed at the ankle. It is preferable not to cross at the knee when you're wearing a dress/skirt.

Sitting with your leg crossed atop your knee takes up space, gives a sloppy impression, and shows how worn out your soles are.

Making the interviewer wait while you to shut down your phone or other tech devices is not the best way to start.

Telephone Interviews

Some studies and body language experts believe that the majority of our communication is nonverbal—through our voice and our expressions—and that only a small percentage of our message is communicated with words.

Here are a few tips when your interview (or any significant call) is via telephone:

- Shower. Brush your teeth. Get dressed. (You don't necessarily have to wear your best suit, but PJs just won't make you feel as confident or professional.)

- Close doors. Turn off phones, music, and any other distracting sounds. (Sorry, but this includes Fido and/or Felix.)

- Stand. This helps your tone of voice and energy level. (Besides, if you sit down, you might be tempted to start browsing online or doodling.)

- Have your résumé/application, pens, notepad, and a glass of water ready. (Don't drink the water while on the call, they'll hear it . . . but just in case you start coughing, you'll have it there.)

- Your monitor, if open at all, should be on the company website.

Virtual Interviews

When you have a video interview, treat it as though you were meeting in person.

Apply all of the suggestions above, and:

- *Do* dress up (even below the waist; you never know if you'll have to stand).
- Sit up straight. Don't recline or put your feet up on your desk. (Wait until you get the penthouse corner office for that.)
- Remove the "hunky fireman calendar" that hangs behind you. Find a location where the backdrop is simple and neat. If necessary, use someone's office.
- Focus on the person. (Look at the camera when you speak.)
- Smile. Don't forget, they can see you at all times.
- Don't doodle, check your phone, or wave to your roommate as he walks by.
- Speak in a normal tone. No need to lean in or exaggerate your lips.

....

WHAT TO WEAR

Professionally Casual

Are there different standards depending on the industry? Does a casual, laid-back work atmosphere lead to an unprofessional attitude and behavior?

Casual Turns Cruddy on Fridays

Have you seen your boss unshaven, seemingly hygiene-deficient, and wearing going-on-three-day-worn jeans with a message themed t-shirt as he strolls into the office on Friday? Or maybe you've seen the tight-fitting capri-style jeggings, crystal encrusted flip-flops or slipper-like boots, randomly pinned-up hair, and cropped pink sweatshirt on a female counterpart? Is that taking "casual Friday" too far?

Consider this:

- What if a client unexpectedly pops in?
- What if a coworker's cute cousin from out-of-town wants to meet you after work?
- What if you're asked to give a last-minute presentation?
- What if you receive a message from "the one you've been waiting for" from your online dating service asking to meet you after work?
- What if you get dismissed by the server at a restaurant because you look like you aren't going to be a good tipper?
- What if your boss's boss asks to see you, take you to lunch, or include you in a meeting?

It's like being prepared for an earthquake—even though you may never have to use it, it's wise to have everything you need to survive for three days.

How you dress sends a message, even if you did not intend it to. Selecting a random, wrinkled, stained, washed-out, or missing-button article of clothing generally sends the message that you don't care, and that's fine. However, it could imply that you don't care about other things or aspects of your life, which can lead to losing business, a promotion, service, or love—even on casual Friday.

> "Eat to please thyself, but dress to please others." —Benjamin Franklin, American statesman, philosopher, and inventor

Dress for the Job You Want.

Cliché, but true (as most clichés are).

Some excuses I've heard for not dressing well:

"I can't afford it." Uh, sorry, there are many bargains to be found if you shop online, watch for sales, or patronize the less expensive stores (like chain markdown stores, outlets, and thrift or consignments shops). Still have no clue what to wear? Look online or ask someone who is up and coming in your field of work.

"No one dresses up at work." Let me get all Mom on you: if everyone jumped off a bridge . . . ? Of course, you don't want to walk around in a three-piece, custom-tailored Italian silk suit if the atmosphere is more along the lines of khakis and polo shirts. However, you can't go wrong dressing a step above everyone else.

"I don't want to attract attention." Why not? If I looked at your personal social media page, would I see a demure and low-key persona who doesn't want to attract attention? Hmm? So what, the first day or two your coworkers will whistle at your stylish duds, but after that, they'll get used it. Besides, it'll be positive attention. They'll wonder what you're up to: a job promotion, a new love interest, or a secret assignment. You may even become an inspiration to them.

> "I dress for the image. Not for myself, not for the public, not for fashion, not for men."—Marlene Dietrich, German actress and singer

What You Wear Tells a Story: What's Yours?

I am not an image consultant; in fact, I've sought their advice. Our clothes typically express our mood and expose a little of who we are or are trying to portray.

Consider this when you reach in your closet or drawer:

Men and Women:

Jeans: (Read company policy.) No visible come-hither embellishments or messages on your booty as you walk away, no rips or lacy patches, and no worn-out bib overalls.

Shoes: No flip-flops (at least not every day). (If something falls on your toe, don't go screaming "disability.") Plus, looking at toes grasping onto a dirty sandal is disgusting and not professional. No sweaty, dirty tennis shoes or glittery slippers, either.

Not to dwell on the flip-flops, but I do get asked to comment on them a lot. While in some workplaces they might be totally adequate, if there was an earthquake or unexpected evacuation, keeping a pair of sturdy shoes in your drawer, locker, or car might be a good idea.

Shorts and Sweats: Just don't.

Also: No wrinkled, torn, dirty, slogan t-shirts (unless it's the company slogan), and reconsider sports team or fashion brands. ("But everyone else wears that stuff." Alright, go ahead and blend right in.)

Q: What's wrong with this picture?

A: Nothing. At least, not in the mind of the "hipster" or whatever trendy label this girl identifies with.

Note: Standing out or making a statement is your choice. However, are you at work to express yourself and make people like you just the way you are (now I can't get that Billie Joel song out my head), or are you there to build a professional reputation? Go ahead and express yourself, but consider toning it down a bit or saving it for the weekend.

"There are two types of people—those who come into a room and say, 'Well, here I am,' and those who come in and say, 'Ah, there you are.'"
—Frederick Collin, American lawyer and politician

Just for Women:

Please avoid mini-skirts, skimpy sundresses, spaghetti straps revealing your bra straps, tight tank tops, halter tops, too much cleavage, and exposed midriff (displaying your darling pelican tattoo). You want them to focus on your brilliant ideas, work ethic, and competence, don't you? No need to swing to the other extreme and dress like a nun. Keep it stylish/trendy with a large dose of conventional.

Just for Men:

Please, can we get over this tired trend? Besides, gentlemen, it does nothing for your silhouette. Dump the saggin' pants. (Come on. Pull them up; buy a belt.) Is there an age cutoff for wearing them like that? I say when you get a job and want to be treated as a professional, the saggin' pants have to go. Just sayin'. Also, avoid mesh shirts or tank-tops and tight-fitting shirts that hug your six-pack (or one-pack).

Conversely, wearing a designer outfit and carrying the latest high-tech gadget will make a wow first impression, but will the suit dim into the background once you open your mouth or walk into the boardroom, taking the seat at the head of the table as you shove a complementary pastry down your throat?

Let's bring back a little style.

Still Not Convinced?

Try this: Gentlemen, go to a department store or tux shop. Try on a suit or tux, with shiny shoes and all. Take a long look in the mirror; just enjoy looking at yourself.

Okay, are you back? How did you feel? Did you stand up a little straighter? Did your left eyebrow lift, giving yourself the "Hey there" look? Did you feel like the most handsome man in the world? Were you surprised that a piece of clothing can give you that much confidence?

Ladies: Do something similar, only make it a chic pantsuit (if you don't like dresses or skirts), an evening dress, or a cocktail dress; include dressy shoes, heels, or nice flats. I'll wait . . .

Our posture, the way we sit, and our attitudes change when we wear certain clothing.

So whatever you choose to wear, wear it proudly. It really comes down to attitude. Put on a smile, have good posture, use tactful words, and maintain a sense of humor; with that combination, you will win most people over.

....

TATTOOS AND OTHER ENHANCEMENTS

From the Audience:

Q: I have this tattoo on my neck that I got a long time ago. I put a big ol' bandage over it when I go to job interviews, but then I'm like, what are they thinking? Do I tell them about it?—Letty

---

Rosalinda Gets Personal:

I'm ashamed to admit this, but it happened. A gentleman approached me. Instinctively, I took a step back as he extended his hand to shake. Not a huge step; not enough for him to notice. Gosh, I wouldn't be that rude! Why, you wonder, did I back away at all? His look. He appeared to be unkempt, with his just-rolled-out-of-bed hair, greasy face, untucked shirt that looked several days worn, and jeans that were obviously too big for him.

We don't mean to judge people. But when we don't know them, our instincts kick in, and we react to them. I expected bed-head boy to be smelly. So, instinctively, I put some space between us. Shameful, but true. Don't be on either side of that encounter.

A: Dear Letty,

Although tattoos have become more mainstream, in some industries there is still reluctance to hire someone with a visible tattoo. This applies to extreme piercings and hair-styles, too.

Slapping a bandage across your neck only calls more attention to it. Also, the interviewer might wonder what is oozing underneath it.

Options:

- If it's small or light in color, use makeup.
- Wear a scarf around your neck or a high-collared shirt.
- Let your hair grow and pull it forward.
- Try laser tattoo removal, if your budget allows.

- Check out the company's tattoo policy before applying.

Letty, once you are called in for a second interview, or if they hire you on the spot, let them know. It wouldn't be honest if you didn't tell them. The exception is, of course, if the company's philosophy is open to visible body art, then you have nothing to worry about. Well, maybe if it's gang-affiliated or blatant cuss words.

Just for Men:

Consider wearing a collared-shirt, hey, maybe even a tie! Or you can help the turtleneck make a comeback. Grow a beard, but keep it maintained.

• • • • •

Q: I'm sick of explaining my tattoo to people. I get it; it's really colorful and pretty. I don't want to be rude to them, but sometimes I don't feel like talking about it. How do I make it stop?—Veneshia

First meeting? Looks like a pleasant chap. How can he upgrade the look? Take his hand out of his pocket and roll down the sleeves. Maybe go the extra mile and wear a tie.

A: Dear Veneshia,

First of all, you can't make people stop from asking. Additionally, how nice that so many people like and are interested in your tattoo. When you wear something cute like shoes, a necklace, or purse, don't people stop and compliment you? Some may even ask you where you bought it. We are intrigued by unique and pretty things. A question is a lot better than a disapproving stare. If you display it, expect people to yea or nay it.

Hey Sagger, Got a Belt?

When did underwear become outerwear? Do what you want around your family and friends, but do you really think your coworkers—or, worse, the people at an interview—need to see your thong or boxers?

If you wear low-rise pants, buy low-rise underwear! Problem solved.

By the way, if your "goods" are on display, people are going to look. And another thing, don't you want people to notice you instead of your underwear?

Just for Women:

This includes bra straps, ladies. Do you really want your coworkers to see your thong, peek-a-boo tattoo, or any other details that could cause them to make conclusions about you and possibly treat you differently? Even if the workplace is open and laid-back, you can decide to show who you are and what you know, instead of what you have and what you show.

Sick and tired of the same old question: What does your tattoo stand for? Here are a few options for you:

- With a smile, say, "Nothing."
- "It signifies [insert your story, or even make one up that's quick to share]."
- Pretend you don't hear them; but that's rude.
- Flash, telling them that you are sick and tired of answering the same ol' question; but that is super rude.
- "Thanks for asking, but it is personal." (Use your nice voice.)
- Look at it as a nice human interaction; you are putting smiles on people's faces.
- Cover it up.

Hats and Shades

Unless it is required for health or safety purpose, please take the hat off! A hat is primarily to protect your head from the sun, rain, snow, or cold. Do you keep your raincoat on once you enter a building? Do you stroll around the warehouse with your umbrella? Do you keep your sunglasses on . . . oh wait. Yes, you do.

There are exceptions, of course, once you get the job. If the atmosphere is ultra casual and a lot of the men wear hats indoors, then go for it.

Just for Men:

Removing one's hat is still considered a sign of respect. You are showing the person your entire face. If you walk into an interview wearing a hat and lookin' all fly, don't be surprised if they ask you to remove it, even in the most casual of industries. And if they don't, you may have just lost the job. Perhaps a slightly exaggerated statement, but showing a little deference and adhering to a tradition shows respect for the occasion.

When can a man keep his hat on? Well, it's a free country, so (technically) you can keep it on whenever you want. But to follow tradition, you may keep your hat on at a birthday party (if it's a party hat), for religious observances, outdoors, and for protection.

Wearing shades indoors is a style; I get it. But what about Shakespeare's quote: "The eyes are the window to the soul." Oh, you don't want to expose your soul? Then remove them because it's kind of peculiar staring at myself in your shades or trying to make eye contact with you.

> It is alleged that hip-hop artists made it fashionable for men to wear their pants low, showing their boxers or briefs. Others say that this style originated in prison, when inmates got their belts taken away. Who really knows or cares? Cities across America have actually proposed ordinances against sagging pants.

From the Audience:

Q: I'm in my 50s, balding, and looking for a job. My wife advised me to wear one of those trendy hats; she said it would make me look younger. I told her that I feel uncomfortable, especially wearing it to a job interview. Can it help?—Todd

A: Dear Todd,

With all due respect to your wife, no. Wearing a hat, no

matter what style, around the house, to the mall, at a base-ball game, etc., is one thing. But please, don't wear a hat to a job interview or a networking event—unless the networking event is casual and being held outdoors.

When your hair growth changes, change the haircut. Try a stylist who can give you a style that helps blend in the balding area. It's not as they won't eventually see your lack of locks.

> Did you know? Men used to tip their hats as a sign of respect, acknowl-edgment, or greeting. Some believe that the origin was from Assyrian times when captives were stripped naked to establish enslavement. [1]

Caught Looking?

Not only does the undie-exposure call attention, but so do pajama bottoms, dirty-looking jeans, shorty-shorts, and crusty-heeled feet.

Look, people can wear what they want; it's their reputa-tion and image. But with a non-mainstream look comes the occasional glance, evil eye, and, unfortunately, even creepy flirtation. Right or wrong, that is reality.

If you get caught looking at the odd or unmentionable garment, apologize. Didn't your mama teach you not to stare?

Making crude comments or providing a lecture on fash-ion is not acceptable. Bite your tongue, or you may end up spending your Saturday in a sexual harassment class.

> Did you know? For centuries, Chinese judges had routinely worn smoke-colored lenses to mask their eye expressions in court. [2]

Your Zipper Is Down.

"Hey, your zipper's down." Common sense dictates that you don't point and make a public announcement. Well, unless you're in a frat house or it's your little brother and you enjoy embarrassing him.

Dilemma: You're in your cubicle, sitting at your workstation when, without notice, your supervisor enters. He stands at the entryway, casually leaning against the partition, chatting away about the upcoming holiday weekend. Nice, right? You happen to notice that his zipper is down. And now, you've tuned him out, hearing only the voice inside your head spinning with possibilities. What do you do?

- Interrupt, "Excuse me, Gary, your zipper."
- Wait until Gary is about to leave, then tell him.
- Tell him to "XYZ" ("examine your zipper" . . . a little too cutesy for the workplace).
- Ignore it, and let someone else tell Gary.

Although the workplace should be gender and culturally neutral, many customs and beliefs are so ingrained that a knee-jerk reaction is predisposed. In addition, cultural differences can create misunderstandings or embarrassing situations.

What if "Gary" was "Jagjit" or "Gilberto Enrique," newly arrived from their respective countries? Don't get all bent out of shape—this is not a radical comment—this is reality in today's workplace. During a presentation, this topic came up. An attorney in the group immediately spoke up, advising everyone not to address anything like this to the opposite sex, no matter what the origins of the person are. "Sexual harass-ment!" he cried out. He advised asking someone of the same sex to speak to the overexposed coworker. Is that taking it a bit too far? You decide, but do use common sense.

Question: How do you handle this dilemma?

Answer: All of the above. If you have an amicable rela-tionship with Gary, Jagjit, or Gilberto Enrique, tell him about his zipper discreetly and matter-of-factly.

As with everything that I write about, I offer options for you to consider, modify, or completely dismiss.

Freely expressing yourself is a wonderful thing; however (you knew that was coming), when you express yourself in your "unique" way, there is a price to pay. You may not like people's reactions, but that's a small price if your "look" or attitude makes you happy. (It sounds as if I'm mocking; sin-cerely, if you believe in your eccentric look, go for it. Reality: some doors will close.)

Is the attention you're seeking, the attention you're getting?

Take a moment to use a mirror to make sure every-thing is in its place.

WRAP-UP

62 Fabulous Tips to Upgrade Your Professional Presence and Build a Sparkling Reputation

1   Arrive on time.

2   End on time.

3   When necessary, apologize (without excuses).

4   Smile.

5   Have a cheerful disposition, no matter what.

6   Stand up straight.

7   Sit up straight.

8   Shower daily.

9   Apply deodorant.

10   Go easy on the cologne.

11   Freshen your breath.

12   Check yourself out in the mirror.

13   Drive courteously (at least in the parking lot).

14   If panicky or grumpy, take a deep breath before entering the workplace.

15   Don't chew gum in public.

16   Iron your clothes.

17   Clean shoes. Clean clothes. Dress the part.

18   Remove pet hair.

19   Don't take your pet to meetings. (But if you do, please control Fi-fi.)

20   Carry a pen and notepad.

21   Don't share too much of your personal life.

22   Greet people.

23   Make eye contact.

24   "Would you like a cup of . . . ?" not, "Can I get you a cup . . . ?"

25   If you have a bad habit, work on it.

26   RSVP!

27   Walk your client to the door.

28   Avoid using curse words and slang.

29   Don't take a call during a meeting.

30   Use "please" and "thank you."

31   Use "You're welcome" instead of "No problem."

32   Don't use the phrase "you guys."

33   If you don't know, say so and then research.

34   Humor, used in moderation, is an effective tool.

35   Pass out genuine compliments.

36   Learn to graciously accept a compliment.

37   Avoid ordering messy menu items.

38   Don't expect everyone to agree with you.

39   Walk away from gossip.

40   Keep your political views private.

41   What will your client see? Monitor your social media page.

42   Seek assistance when necessary.

43   Acknowledge those who guide you.

44   Answer your phone in a calm and pleasant tone.

45   Return calls and emails promptly.

46   Learn to shake hands.

47   Pause, giving others a chance to speak.

48   Maintain a comfortable distance.

49   Limit "touching."

50   Don't lecture a smoker.

51   Listen to your gut, even if it means losing a client.

52   Don't talk only about business; find a hobby.

53   If you aren't enjoying what you do, it will be obvious.

54   Life is too short for misunderstandings to linger; privately speak to the person, maintaining a respectful tone, and move on.

55   Say "Yes" instead of "Yeah."

56   Speak kindly about others.

57   The correct term is an "invitation," not an "invite."

58   Remember: not your office, not your rules.

59   Keep aromatic leftovers at home—not in the office.

60   At your breaking point? Stop and reschedule, take a walk, or drink a glass of water.

61   Wait or return later, but don't interrupt.

62   Fine-tune your table manners.

It's your choice, whether you want to climb the ladder, stay where you are, or make a lateral move, why not do it with professionalism and a forward-looking attitude? It is your reputation, after all.

CHAPTER 2

HYGIENE

PLEASE COVER YOUR MOUTH—JUST DO.

Try to suppress a yawn. Impossible. You may think you did, but everyone around you knows you yawned.

Suppressing a yawn only makes your face contort—which, by the way, is more conspicuous than allowing the yawn to do its thing.

> Why should you care? Singly, an open-mouthed yawn, a finger up your nose, or satisfying an armpit itch isn't going to tarnish your image, but collectively, it paints a picture of who you are and what your ideals of conduct are. If you are content in your station or apathetic to those around you, itch, pick, and yawn away.

Here are some yawning pointers when in the company of others:

- Cover your mouth.
- When possible, slightly turn your head to one side.
- No roars, grunts, or languishing sighs. Keep it down.
- Don't intentionally extend the yawn. I know it feels good, but sometimes you've got to cut it short.
- A whispered "pardon me" is a nice gesture.
- Unless it is a close friend, don't bother sharing your tired story about the amorous cats that kept you up all night.
- A brief, but sincere, "I'm sorry" is recommended if you yawn right in front of somebody's face.
- If you are the beholder of a yawn, please refrain from saying, "Oh, am I boring you?" or "Sorry, am I keeping you up?" I know it's said to ease the awkward moment, but it just makes the yawner feel worse (especially if you really are boring).

> Did you know? People of the Middle Ages believed the devil entered your mouth through a yawn, so it was important to cover your mouth or make the sign of the cross over your mouth. [3]

....

SNEEZING

From the Audience:

Q: When someone sneezes, I automatically say, "Bless you," even if I don't know them. I've been told that some people might be offended by this. But I'm just trying to be nice.
—Travis

A: Dear Travis,

I'm not sure why some people are offended when someone wishes good things upon them.

Hearing the entire phrase "God bless you" can set some people off. If you see that your coworker is uncomfortable with that phrase, use the ever-popular "Gesundheit." Maybe we can adopt the Russian phrase *bud zdrov* ("be healthy") or the Chinese *bai sui* ("may you live 100 years." They can't be offended by something they don't understand . . .).

When I discussed this topic with preteens, they came up with some points that made sense, to them and to me:

If a person doesn't believe in God, why are they offended by something they don't believe exists?

If someone doesn't really know if they believe in God, a "blessing" can't hurt . . . it's just something nice to say.

Consider this: Have you ever been told to "go to hell" by anyone? What if you don't believe in hell? Would you be offended that they mentioned a place you don't believe in or would you think of their intent? Ultimately, it's a rude thing to say, but is it worth becoming offended?

It is rude to turn away a well-meaning wish. Say, "Thank you," and be glad that someone took notice of you. Life is too short to let a "Bless you" bother you.

> If you're a "sneezer," carry along tissue or a hanky (they actually still sell them). Use your left hand to cover your mouth. Turn away from others while you sneeze. If your sneezes are "sickly" and contagious, stay home, please.

Sick?

What crosses your mind when Alejandro, who works next to you on the line, is hacking and rubbing his nose all day? *Gross!* That's probably followed by a few other unkind thoughts, right?

If you're sick, please stay home. Most employers and coworkers prefer it. Oh, you feel guilty? Stay later or go in earlier when you return to work.

Going to work when you're ill or contagious is commendable? And conscientious? The choice to infect everyone will not reflect favorably on your decision-making process. (There are always exceptions.)

Sick Because of Poor Decisions?

Bragging and/or whining about last night's binge does not do anything for your professional reputation. Keep it to yourself. Oh, sure, your work buddies might laugh and joke with you about it, but, when it comes down to it, would you be the one they'd want to travel with to the next conference? Or invite to their home?

P.S. Remove the pictures of last night's merriment from your social media page ASAP!

> Loud or silent, burps smell! And when you don't acknowledge it, it makes the rest of us wonder what else you'll be releasing and pretending you didn't.

The Puffed-Cheek Burp Is Still a Burp.

"I can't hold a good burp in." In most cases, yes, you can. If you are alone, go for it.

But when you're not alone, consider these tips:

- In your car, you're not really "alone." People can see your gaping mouth as you release the belch. Why should you care? Well, it could be a cute girl who was ready to flirt with you. It could be your neighbor. It could be the person who will be interviewing you for a job.
- Don't exaggerate the burp.
- Don't try to impress anyone with how well you can burp-talk (except maybe your sixth-grade nephew).
- Think you can get away with it because we are walking side by side; I might look up right at that moment . . . smelly, remember?
- Don't try to hide it. Your cheeks will puff up like a squirrel with acorns, and then you'll blow it out. Gross.

- If it slips, simply say, "Pardon me, please." And move on.

Did you know? Generally, burping is caused by the air that we swallow. A few culprits are smoking, chewing gum, sipping through a straw, eating too fast, and wearing loose dentures.

Need a reason to say no to veggies? Some of the burp-inducers are cauliflower, broccoli, onions, artichokes, and asparagus. [4]

Breaking Wind. Just Don't!

Loud or silent, flatulence smells!

If I'm alone, can I let 'er rip? Sure. Psst, standing alone in the aisle at the grocery store does not count.

From the Audience:

Q: I've got a medical condition that makes it difficult to control breaking wind. It is especially awkward at networking events. What can I do so that I don't offend anyone?—Benny

A: Dear Benny,

I'll try not to sound flippant about this.

- If you can, stand close to a doorway or window.
- Wear a jacket that is long and buttons; this can contain the odorous gases.
- Attempt to expel as much as possible in the restroom to eliminate the frequency or intensity.
- Stand behind a table or chair to create more space between you and other people.

I hope this helps.

"You did not fart, you did not burp; didn't you like the meal?"—allegedly Martin Luther, German Reformer. However, there's no real proof of it. (The German version: *"Warum furzet und rülpset ihr nicht? Hat es euch nicht geschmecket?"*)

Bibiana Pops In

Picture it: You are in your cubicle, not expecting anyone, so you release some pent-up gas. Then, out of nowhere, Bibiana pops in. Uh-oh! Will she notice? Of course she will!

"Stop! I'm contagious!"

Here are some options:

- Quickly get up and tell her you were just on your way to the [insert any destination]. Have the conversation on the way to the made up destination or just outside your cubicle.

- Before Bibiana sits down, look really stressed and tell her that you can't talk; you'll have to see her later. Look down at "whatever," don't look back, and hope she walks away. This may or may not work.

- Honesty is the best policy—own it. "I'm so sorry; I'm having a little trouble with my stomach today. Why don't we go down to your office?"

If you are going to Malawi in southeast Africa, don't cut the cheese. They are resurrecting a "public decency" law that classifies farting in public as pollution. [5]

Bad Breath

Garlic, Onions, Curry, Tuna, Coffee, Alcohol, and Cigarettes: A Few Potent Culprits That Keep People at Bay

Do you ever wonder about your breath? I do—I wonder whether what I've eaten lingers or not.

Bad breath can cause a distraction during a conversation. I know that I've had to step back to avoid inhaling the lingering aroma of the pesto-garlic slathered sandwich someone had for lunch.

Ah, mints, you say; what a practical solution. Sucking on or chewing a mint can also be distracting to the person with whom you are speaking. They'll be mesmerized by your tongue's agility to move the melting mint from side to side.

How about a piece of peppermint chewing gum? Chewing? Again, a distraction for the onlooker. Chewing gum in public is a no-no.

Next. Parsley is supposed to work. Just make sure that you pop into the restroom to look in the mirror; the little greenery may get stuck between your teeth.

I prefer using a pocket mist or breath strips. No hassle, no mess, out of sight. All anyone will notice is the freshness of your breath.

Rosalinda Gets Personal:

During a dance lesson, one of the instructors had putrid alcohol breath—and guess who he used as an example partner? At the break, students and teacher alike stood in a circle. This was my only opportunity, so I whipped out my breath mints and offered them to everyone in class. Everyone accepted, except for the icky-breath instructor.

There is another option: Don't eat pungent foods when you know that you will be networking, working closely with someone on a project, anticipating an intimate evening, or going on a job interview. Simple. Enjoy your whiffy fare another time.

Beware of savory foods. Your breath's appeal, or lack of it, is as much a part of grooming as wiping the goo from your eyes. Being aware of your breath is a considerate thing to do. It really is to your benefit. With bad breath, they'll step back; with fresh breath, they'll come in a little closer.

Take special consideration about your breath if you are a dentist/hygienist, hair stylist, make-up artist, eyebrow threader, or work in any other industry that requires face-to-face time.

Death Breath

From the Audience:

Q: Help! I've got a coworker whose breath is just atrocious! We work for a small company, and even worse, we work side-by-side. I don't know what his problem is, but every morning his breath just about knocks me down. Break time is better because by then he's got coffee breath—still bad, but better. I like the guy, but I don't know if I can stand by him another day. What can I do?—Don

A: Dear Don,

Ask for a transfer. Wear a face mask. Rub lavender oil above your upper lip. Have a bowl of mints at your workstation. (I'll bet that every other guy in the place will take one except him!)

Your coworker's bad breath could be caused by gum disease, diabetes, tooth decay, poor hygiene, medications, or several other possible reasons. The worst part is your coworker may not even be aware of it.

If you have a friendly relationship with him, approach him privately. To ease the tension, sometimes I take the "I-had-this-problem-too" path. This way you aren't pointing out his dilemma, instead you are *sharing* the torment of his dilemma. Explain that you were grateful when someone took you aside, so you are doing the same. You may learn that he has an ailment—if he does, go back to my initial

recommendations. If he isn't aware, he will be now.

Another route is to speak to the HR department and let them handle it.

Oh, You're a Smoker?

Please don't skip this because you hate anything smoker-related. While I don't promote smoking, I'm not an anti-smoking fanatic.

> Employers must and do consider the health-related costs; smokers tend to take more frequent and longer breaks making them less productive, hence peeving coworkers, not to mention the lingering scent.

Dear Smokers,

You already have a bad rap; don't give non-smokers more to lecture you about. Consider this:

- Don't take excessive smoke-breaks. What's excessive? More than your non-smoking co-workers take. I know, I know, smoking your ciggy is supposed to be relaxing. But you're at work; make it quick.

- Does this habit hurt your chances for a promotion?

- Before re-entering the building, air yourself out. Don't walk down the hall exhaling the last puff.

- If you are in a crowded area, wait or walk away. Naturally, follow all of the posted "designated smoking areas." Others won't be bothered, and you can enjoy your ciggy in peace.

- Asking, "Do you mind if I smoke?" is a nice gesture.

- After a disapproving glare or comment, either don't acknowledge it or calmly reply, "I'm trying to quit" (even if you aren't) or "I'll be out of your way soon." Just because they are rude doesn't mean you have to be.

- Don't flick your butt! Dispose of it properly.

> "To some, the cigarette is a portable therapist."—Terri Guillemets, American quote anthologist

Dear Non-Smokers,

Yes, we all know that smoking is bad for one's health; smokers know it, too. Consider this:

- Do not ask a smoker why they smoke. Why do you drink coffee? See, it's none of your business.

- You do not have the right to lecture a smoker about the dangers of smoking, the ozone layer, second-hand smoke, etc.

- When sharing a space with a smoker, you have two choices: move away or politely ask them to extinguish their ciggy. Unless there is a posted sign, they have as much right to be there as you do.

- Do not grab their ciggy, toss it on the ground, and stomp on it. You may have to reimburse them for that.

- Do not dramatize hacks and coughs as you walk by a smoker. It makes you look silly.

- And those glaring stares as you walk by them—stop it. It's rude and unbecoming. Besides, they aren't breaking any laws.

- A little tolerance, please. A hint of second-hand smoke may annoy you, but it certainly won't cause permanent damage.

Rosalinda Gets Personal:

I love smelling a lit cigarette while garlic slowly sizzles in olive oil on the stove. The combination evokes heartwarming memories of my grandparents' home. On occasion, I'll light a cigarette while cooking garlic in olive oil. (I'm glad to report that no one in my home was harmed or has suffered from this practice.)

Flossing Flo

From the Audience:

Q: Our company recently restructured our workstations; there are now two people to a cubicle. I share my cubicle with "Flo." The problem begins when Flo returns from lunch. Sitting in her chair, she whips around and faces me, talking and flossing. From time to time, I see a bit of food fly out of her mouth. The last straw was when a chunk landed on my shoe. How do I stop this?—Raul

"So, what did you have for lunch?"

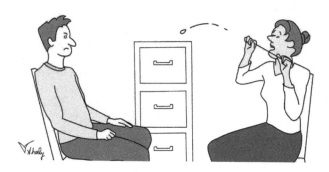

A: Dear Raul,

Pardon me for a moment . . . Okay, I believe I'm through heaving now. Not only do those pesky morsels land all over the place, but her fingers are full of her saliva. Got hand sanitizer?

Any type of grooming, especially in front of a coworker, is a little too cozy. Here are a few phrases you might consider using:

"I have a sensitive stomach; do you mind flossing in the restroom?"

"Do you mind facing your wall? I'm easily grossed out. Thanks."

"(chuckling) Flo, I think you'd better floss somewhere

Privately prepare "guidelines" (for your eyes only) of topics and things that bug you about your cube-buddy. Some items may include voice level, eating, phone call privacy, music, visitors, perfume, all grooming-related topics, boundaries for borrowing, and any other matters that are of concern. End it on a high note: If anything comes up for either one of us, let's agree to discuss it and keep it between us.

else . . . I found a piece of your lunch stuck on my shoe yesterday."

"I'm so used to having a private space that I have to remind myself that I'm not alone. Flo, I apologize if I've done anything to gross you out or annoy you. You know, this might be a good time to talk about some guidelines."

The Unwashed Colleague

From the Audience:

Q: What do you do when you see a coworker walk out of the bathroom without washing his or her hands?—Jeffrey

He's the guy that handed me a bagel this morning!

A: Dear Jeffrey,

I probably wouldn't want shake his hand, accept an unwrapped sandwich from him, or use his cell phone. What remains is the haunting image of creepy crawly bathroom bacteria on their hands, and the impulse to alert everyone in the office. However, if you hadn't actually seen him exit the restroom, you would never have thought about it.

Thankfully, we humans are pretty hearty. We probably consume and touch many things that would make us shudder.

The best recourse is to do or say nothing—and I mean to anyone. (Good luck with that!)

Options: You can bring up the subject at the next meeting; print and laminate a picture of soapy hands and place it inside the stall, on the exit door or bathroom mirror; anonymously place a bottle of hand-sanitizer on his desk; or covertly bring the subject up in conversation: "I was at a restaurant last week and actually saw this guy walk out without washing his hands; do people still do that? . . . With so much bacteria all over the place, colds, etc., you just wonder what they're thinking." Too thespian-like? Well, you can adjust it to suit your personality.

Just for Men:

At the risk of becoming too graphic, in reality, you require a more thorough hand-washing than your female counterpart. Ahem, you require direct contact with your body, while a woman can easily maneuver without doing so. So, in reality, it is worse seeing a man walk out without soaping up! Thank you.

Bathroom Chit Chat

From the Audience:

Q: When using the restroom, there are some coworkers who, without apprehension, continue the conversation while in the stall; I find it awkward to chit chat while conducting my "business." What can I do to stop the chatter?—Thomas

> Did you know? Erasmus of Rotterdam, a sixteenth-century scholar, wrote one of the first recorded etiquette books. Here is what he said about manners in the bathroom: "It is impolite to greet someone who is urinating or defecating." On breaking wind, he says, "Let a cough hide the explosive sound a replace farts with coughs." [6]

A: Dear Thomas,

As you enter the stall, say something brief like, "I'll finish telling you in a minute." If your coworker is doing the talking, you can cut him off by saying, "Tell me the rest in a minute," or "I'll meet you out here; you can tell me then." Find a stall at the opposite end. If the chatter continues, don't reply or you can flush for noise-blocking purposes. And with a matter-of-fact tone, pick up where you left off as you exit the restroom.

P.S. The company restroom is a risky place to share private stuff.

KEY POINTS:

- Yawning: Using your left hand to cover your mouth. Subtly turn away. Say, "Pardon me, please."

- Burps: Hold it or cover it. If unavoidable, subtly turn away and say, "Pardon me, please."

- Passing gas: Take a walk outside or take it to the bathroom. If it happens in front of someone, say "I'm sorry. Please, pardon me," and keep it moving. Ask them to join you for a walk.

- Smoking at work: Keep breaks to a minimum, make up your time, and air yourself out!

- Grooming (of any kind): Please handle it in private (even if you think you and your co-worker are chums).

- Shower regularly, and change your clothes regularly.

- Breath: Be considerate of others. Brush, rinse, or mint!

- If you are sick, please stay home.

- Wash your hands, please.

CHAPTER 3

TELEPHONE, SOCIAL MEDIA, AND ELECTRONICS

(Tweets, Likes, and the Like)

These non-face-to-face methods of communication are practical and quick, but because of the often spontaneous nature of these methods of communication, confusion, embarrassment, and disputes can arise.

The next time you are feverishly typing a message, bear in mind that, except for a phone call (unless, unbeknownst to you, it is being recorded), your words will hang around for eternity. Egads!

DOES YOUR TONE MAKE ME WANT TO HANG UP?

It seems redundant to address the topic of the telephone, but with so many people complaining about it, I thought it was worth commenting on.

Let's start with the basics. The way you answer the phone or text can determine the way I perceive you. Yes, my perception may be wrong, but that's all I have to go on.

Bottom line: don't treat your professional calls like you do your personal ones. Or go ahead, but if a potential employer calls you and hears the lyrics to "Take This Job and Shove It," or a flippant message like, "Hey, I must be out, so give a shout," the impression may not be too favorable.

The difference between a positive and negative experience with a phone call is your voice. How you say "Hello" will set the tone for the conversation. In the business world, this could mean losing a customer or leaving a pretty bad impression with the boss.

At work, no matter what mood you are in, it is your job to answer the telephone in an enthusiastic, charming, and welcoming manner—even if you are starving and just about to take a massive bite of your extra-spicy polish sausage!

Unless you are the company operator, you do have a choice to let the call go to voicemail. Don't overuse this function. Use it when you are feeling disgruntled from the

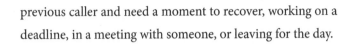
previous caller and need a moment to recover, working on a deadline, in a meeting with someone, or leaving for the day.

Who calls whom? It's quite impractical for two parties to place the call at the same time; it's a time waster and it's awkward.

If you requested the meeting, you make the call. Be clear about it:

"I'll give you a call at 11:00."

"You may expect my call at 11:00."

If you want them to call (for whatever reason):

"I'll expect your call at 11:00."

"I'll let my staff know that you'll be calling at 11:00."

8 More Telephone Tips:

1   Smile when you answer the phone. (Yes, they can tell, and it helps you sound nicer.)

2   Pick up by the third ring (when possible).

3   Speak slowly and calmly and enunciate—every time. (Mumbling, "HithisisRyaninfinance" will only force me to ask you to repeat yourself . . . slow down!)

4   Include the department and your name.

5   If you must put a caller on hold to answer another call, return within ten seconds. Do not handle the new caller first.

6   Don't answer in a frantic or disturbed voice. (It's not the caller's fault that you dislike answering the telephone or that they interrupted your lunch.)

> ### Rosalinda Gets Personal:
>
> Years ago, I had a boss who, from time to time, would call in just to hear how I answered the phone. Naturally, I did my best, so he was never disappointed. What would your boss learn if he conducted a random call-in?

7   Don't eat, drink, chew gum, let out a tired sigh, play computer games, or whisper to your cubicle mate. The caller will pick up on the inattentiveness. (*Uh-huh, yeah-yeah, ohhh, mmm* . . . all indicators that you're not really listening.)

8   Phrases like these can sound curt (especially if the tone in your voice is less than sweet), so find more pleasant alternatives:

NOT: "Wait a minute" or "Hold on."
Preferred: Would you please hold for a moment? (Wait for response)

NOT: "Who's this?"
Preferred: "May I ask who's calling, please?"

NOT: "She's not here."
Preferred: "I'm sorry, but Ms. Cory is not in. May I take a message for her?"

NOT: "Can you call back later?"
Preferred: "I'd be happy to take a message" or "Would you like to call back later?"

NOT: "We're busy right now." (Are you kidding me?! Of course you're busy; you're working, right! Never, ever use this phrase.)

Preferred: If you must communicate this message because you genuinely cannot respond to the caller's

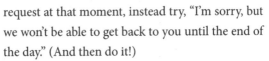

request at that moment, instead try, "I'm sorry, but we won't be able to get back to you until the end of the day." (And then do it!)

NOT: "I don't know." (It makes you sound incompetent! It's okay not to have all the answers; just be sure to find out for next time, or refer them to someone who does know.)

Preferred: "I'm not sure. Would you please hold while I find out for you?" Or, "I can take your number and call you back when I have the information."

Voicemail

Returning a Message: Listen to the entire message before you call back. It'll frustrate the caller to have to repeat it, and it wastes time when you call without being prepared. It kind of says, "I'm too busy to be bothered . . . just tell me what you want."

Leaving a Message: Leave your first and last name (no cutesy nicknames in a business setting), keep it brief, speak clearly and calmly, smile while you record it, use a friendly tone, and avoid or remove background noises.

Speaker Phone

The only reason to place someone on speaker is for your convenience, so that you can continue texting, eating, or checking for vacation deals. (You get the mockery, right?)

Don't place personal calls on speaker phone.

Speak in a regular voice; if the caller can't hear you, they'll tell you.

Always pick up the phone first. (Auto-speaker says, "I'm

Uh-huh . . . ("*Ooh, this is it . . . honeymoon.*") Yeah, I'm still here. . . . interesting . . .

way too busy for you." Besides, they may not want to be announced.)

Always, and beforehand, inform the caller that they are being placed on speaker.

Keep your activities to a minimum; rustling of papers, whispers, and unwrapping a bagel is distracting to the person on the other end.

Placing the caller on speaker is convenient when you have a third (or more) party participating in the call. In such cases, inform the caller who is present or allow the others to introduce themselves. (Say your name when you speak—remember, they can't see you.)

If possible, take all speaker phone calls in a conference room. (The entire department doesn't have to endure your call.)

The Cell Phone (a Blessing and a Curse)

There is nothing more annoying than hearing someone jabber in public or, worse, in the cubicle next to you. It's of no interest to others how cheap your boyfriend is, how the girl

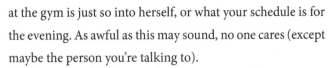
at the gym is just so into herself, or what your schedule is for the evening. As awful as this may sound, no one cares (except maybe the person you're talking to).

No matter how hard your cube-neighbor tries to tune you out, the distraction is there.

Perception of public cell phone user addicts: You are desperate to look important, be listened to, and feel needed. You believe that everyone else's life is so pathetic and dull that listening to yours will be a treat.

Four requests if you must chat in public:

1   Please keep it brief.
2   Please keep it low.
3   Please keep it "G" rated.
4   Please move to the side ('cuz you don't seem to notice there are other people around).

Is "You can't tell me what to do!" running through your mind right now? My response is, no, I cannot tell you what to do, nor am I presuming to tell you what to do. I am merely making an observation. Go ahead and invade my space if you want to.

Think about this: if you're jabbering on your cell phone, how can you wish me a "Good morning" or say "After you" as we enter the coffee shop, or "Thank you" when I've held the elevator for you? Get off the phone, pretty please!

> A public cell phone talker creates a barrier to life.

On-the-Road Cell Phone Meetings and Conversations

If your job keeps you on the road most of the day, you probably have to hold a meeting or two while driving. While it can be a time-saver, especially for brief conversations like confirming an appointment, alerting a client that you are running late, or answering a quick follow-up question, please be aware that it can be a danger to you and inconsiderate to the person on the other end of the phone.

Some important things to consider when scheduling an on-the-road call:

- If you know that you'll be making or accepting a call while driving, be sure to inform the person in advance.

- Offer to schedule the call at a time when you are in your office. (It's a thoughtful gesture.)

- Try not to schedule a first-time meeting while on the road. Getting to know someone requires our full attention.

- Avoid an on-the-road call if it is detail-oriented or significant. Can you really focus on the details or take notes when you are supposed to be focused on driving?

- If you are aware of where the "drop-zone" is, stop the conversation and inform the person that you'll call them back. (You don't want them going on and on assuming that you're listening, do you?)

- If the connection is horrible, apologize and ask

them when you could call them back.

- If you are familiar and friendly with this client/
  colleague, you can be a little more relaxed. "Oh,
  I wish you could see the snow-covered moun-
  tains—they are stunning." They may or may not
  appreciate it. It's your *call*.

- Consider that they can hear the sound of you gulp-
  ing down your smoothie, applying your lipstick,
  chewing and licking your fingers from eating
  your breakfast burrito, or a sudden outburst as
  you yell, "Learn how to drive, you moron!"

Are There Texting Boundaries?

From the Audience:

Q: I find it somewhat unprofessional to text, unless it's a familiar coworker or an on-the-go, long-term client. When
I leave a voicemail and the person responds with a text, it
seems like a boundary has been crossed—too familiar, too
quick. Am I just old-fashioned?—Charlize

A: Dear Charlize,

Texting is great; however, so much can be lost or misunderstood. Incomplete sentences, abbrevd wrds, and lack of
adjectives cannot possibly convey what the sender means.

My guidelines: If the person requests a text to confirm an
appointment, late arrival, or change in location, that is acceptable. However, if we just became acquainted or you are
my company's accountant, attorney, probation officer, or another relationship of similar stature, I would not want to text

anything of consequence. Have you heard of the "text gone wrong"?

So what do you do when you want to discourage a texting conversation? Respond with a brief text:

"I will send you a more extensive reply via email."

"Why don't we schedule a time to talk? Are you available tomorrow?"

"To avoid a lengthy text, may I call you instead?"

"If you don't mind, I prefer communicating via email."

"My cell phone's battery is low; I'll reply from my computer." (a little white lie)

When sending a text, maintain business hours.

IM/Texting. Even though lack of punctuation or an overload of !, :), caps, and abbrevs, are the norm . . . try 2 keep it a bit more profesh. Especially with the boss, a client, or potential employer. P.S. Check it before you send it. (In one text-gone-wrong, I was apparently "taking a bath with Nina.")

....

EMAIL
CORRESPONDENCE

Correspondence via email can be tricky. Without the gestures we use in real life and even the tone we use on the phone, many nuances can be lost.

Letter writing allowed us to rethink and reconsider our words before sending. If the situation is contrary or all-important, you might give it a couple of hours before responding.

Consider these tips:

- Remember: What you read isn't always what they mean. A misunderstanding can be blamed on the perception of a word, skimming through and missing key words, the writer's choice of words, or underdeveloped sentences—all valid.

Rosalinda Gets Personal:

On one occasion, I received news about a consequential schedule change. How did I *react*? Well, shamefully, my emotions took over, which were reflected in the email that I sent out in the heat of the moment. Should I have waited a few hours or a day to respond, I wouldn't have had to send a note apologizing for my emotional and fiery delivery. Etiquette: respond instead of react.

- Read the correspondence twice (without distractions) before reacting.
- If it seems too good, too confusing, too much, too generous, too snarky . . . ask for clarification before jumping to concrete conclusions.
- Once the thread gets too long, feel free to delete portions (keeping only the most recent) or start a new email.
- If it is of great importance or a delicate matter, schedule a phone call (have the information in question in front of you).
- Be prepared to accept the sender's interpretation. (Take the high road and accept it. You can

sit there and doubt their explanation, or you can apologize for misunderstanding it and move on.)

- In addition, if you're going to be corresponding back and forth, please pick up the phone or walk over to their office. You'll have a better chance of resolving the matter more quickly and with less possibility of misinterpretation.

- Always read the entire email. You'll look silly asking about something that was already addressed because you only skimmed through. (Oops! Guilty.)

- Treat email correspondence as you would a business letter.

- Use full sentences and proper grammar.

- Avoid abbrevd & Twitter-style wrds. And, don't #ramble.

- Please use a clear subject line. Howdy, Hi, Just me, or You gotta read this! Not advisable, unless it's your pal. (It could also look like spam.)

- Don't use the "bcc" unless you are in some type of litigation or investigation . . . please check with HR regarding your company's policy. If sending a large group email, and the people involved do not know each other, "bcc" should be considered.

- My opinion is that if you are sending an email to a person who ranks higher than you, or you have just met them, it is a nice touch to address them with a "Dear," and close with the more formal and traditional "Very truly yours" or the little less

formal "Sincerely." Follow their lead on this one.

- If there are details to cover, schedule a phone call.

Still not sure why you should care about sprucing up your electronic communication style? Well, if developing a professional reputation isn't at the top of your list, then perhaps thinking about whose inbox your email can end up in will help you reconsider.

Email Address

"Cupcakelover@xxxmail.com" Cutesy, sexy call names might be fine for your personal email name, but not for business. Just use your name. (Create a separate account for business-related correspondence.)

Email Replies

Do you like to be left hanging? It really is rude not to reply. Besides, if you don't reply within a day or two, it'll get buried and you'll forget about it. If you are busy, write a short note to acknowledge that you received the email and will be communicating again with more information later on. Keep a log book for follow-up.

If you've overlooked an email (it happens), call or reply, simply apologize, and take care of it. That's better than hoping it'll go away.

Rotten reasons for not replying:

"I didn't have the answer." (And I'm supposed to guess that? Send me a note, "I'm working on it . . . " Something!)

"I've been busy." (Uh, me too!)

It is polite to reply within twenty-four hours; however, you have for-ty-eight. You'll find that because of immediate access (cell phone) to messages, most people now expect an immediate response. Patience people, yours isn't the only email in my inbox.

"I thought someone was already handling it." (a.k.a.: an assumption, a guess. Although this one is understandable, it still doesn't quite get the job done.)

"He never replies to my emails . . . make him wait." (A bit immature, don't you think?)

"I am not interested." (So, tell me! Besides, if you don't, I'll only keep sending you stuff. And please don't say that you're afraid to hurt my feelings—it's business. Say it tactfully and politely—there, done!)

If the inquiry or offer is unsolicited, an impersonal mass mailing, or you've told them that you aren't interested for the fifth time, you don't need to reply; just hit "delete" or "unsubscribe."

When you reply to an email, don't reply with half-sen-tences like, "Of course," "You got it!" "Sounds good," or any phrase that comes across as flippant. That is, unless (there are always exceptions) you have been going back and forth with a coworker; after a few emails, formalities can be set aside. This includes salutations and closings.

....

YOUR PROFESSIONAL SOCIAL MEDIA IMAGE

There are some useful practices that you may want to consider when it comes to social media—especially if you are looking for new clients or a new job. And you certainly do not want to give your current company a reason to all of a sudden eliminate your position.

Admittedly, I am not a social media expert. Common sense is the tool I use to make the following recommendations to protect your reputation on social media networks.

Here are the top four things to keep in mind when posting on professional networks:

1   Upload a current and professional-looking photo ("professional" being key). A photo of you holding your adorable kitty cat, you and a friend sitting in a pool bar in Vegas, or a selfie getting ready for a night out with the girls does not fall under that category (unless your job is selling

timeshares in Vegas, or cat-sitting).

2   Keep your posts clean and free from any spicy poses or activities that would raise eyebrows. (This can be difficult to determine since it is all relative. If you're unsure, go with your gut, or ask someone in your field.)

3   Research and share relevant links related to job search, résumé building, etc. (Don't post the location of your favorite bar or shopping boutique. And BTW, limit acronyms, smiley faces, and photos of your recently purchased iced double-pump mocha.) Again, depending on the situation, a note or photo about your personal life can give others a taste of who you are; make that taste tasteful.

4   Keep it civil. If you disagree with someone's comment, ignore it. If you must address it, wait a day (hopefully you'll forget about it). Guard your reputation by choosing your tone (no caps, bold, or too much punctuation) and words carefully. (This is not a time to rant, lecture, or prove someone wrong.)

You're Tagged

Photos were taken at the meeting or business event and posted on social media for everyone to see. And there you are,

> Pretend you're on camera from the moment you step out of your home until you step back in and close the door behind you.

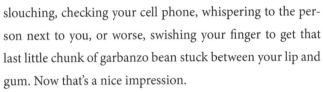

slouching, checking your cell phone, whispering to the person next to you, or worse, swishing your finger to get that last little chunk of garbanzo bean stuck between your lip and gum. Now that's a nice impression.

If you aren't pleased with the caught-on-camera photo, contact the photographer and request that they remove the photo. Most people will understand and comply. If they refuse, ask that they at least "untag" you.

How to Connect

If you see someone who works at a particular company that you are interested in, send them a private message, introduce yourself, and ask them about the company culture—that is a way to begin a conversation without being too forward. If you do not receive a reply, move on.

Do not point-blank ask someone to "get" your résumé to the right person—especially when they don't even know you. Instead of saying, "Can you..." try, "I am looking for a position . . . do you have any suggestions?" (Please and thank you.) This way the person won't feel obligated. They may ignore you, contact you, or come up with some polite excuse.

Just because you receive a request to "connect" does not mean you have to accept. If someone insists, you can politely decline. Remember to handle it with tact. My decision to decline or simply ignore a request is often based on an unprofessional experience that I've had with the person. I might also decline if I see that they are gathering connections only to sell me stuff.

When you receive a request, especially from someone you have never met, try to follow up with a private message thanking them for reaching out. If you have mutual connections, mention that as well. If there could be a mutual collaboration or interest, ask them a question about their field, company, position . . . and the relationship is established. Yes, this takes time, so we can't always reply.

When a potential client or employer looks through your social media sites, don't you want them to get the right impression of you and your business?

Rosalinda Gets Personal:

I received a request to connect from a woman I did not know. I left the request there for a month or so until I had time to look her up and decide whether I wanted to be connected. (Wow, that kind of sounds snobby.) I "accepted" her request, which brought on a lengthy tongue-lashing. She went on and on about the length of time it took me to respond and how she'd have to think about connecting with me now. Sweetheart, take all the time you need, 'cuz guess what? You will now be "declined," forever, from all of my social media links!

Here are a few key points to making contacts and developing relationships:

- Be suave and civil.
- Do not pester someone if they do not respond or if they decline to connect.

- Don't take a "decline to connect" personally.
- If they agree to share your résumé or provide you with any information or leads, always send a

private thank-you message.

- Maintain a positive attitude. If you are in a grumpy mood or are feeling discouraged, don't post that day.

- Offer to help others. Refer and recommend. Share an interesting link.

- If you join a group, take a minute to peruse prior posts before leaving a comment. (If it's been said . . .)

- Take time to "like" other people's comments. This shows others that it isn't all about you.

....

YOUR PERSONAL SOCIAL MEDIA IMAGE

Companies, potential clients, colleagues, a love interest, and even Mom and Dad could run across your personal social media pages. Blah, blah, blah, you've heard it before. Why do you think etiquette experts, HR directors, headhunters, and business coaches keep repeating it? Because it really does matter. You can disagree, consider it unfair, or say that it's nobody's business what you post, but the fact of the matter is, your social media pages will reflect on your image.

I get it. It's your personal life and what you do on your time . . . again, blah, blah, blah! *Au contraire, mon ami.* If it's out there, it becomes everyone's business. People will draw conclusions from what they perceive to be true, and their perception is their reality.

Things to consider:

- Don't assume they don't care about your social media image.

- Don't assume they won't care because it's a "chill" company atmosphere.

- Don't assume they will get your sarcastic morose sense of humor, or like it.

- Don't assume your coworkers won't look.

Rosalinda Gets Personal:

A couple of years ago I was hired by a twenty-something-year-old male to help him polish his dining and business etiquette skills to prepare him for upcoming interviews. At one interview, he was asked about his social media page which he had unpublished several months prior. The interviewer asked him to log in, and he did. The interviewer scrolled three-four years back and didn't like what he saw. Fast forward, he didn't get the job due to unsavory, non-pc, college-day posts which were all done in fun, of course. It *will* haunt you.

If you have an entry-level job, a going-nowhere job, a my-company-can't-live-without-me kind of attitude, or are job hunting, I hope you like job hunting—you might just find yourself in that position for a long time. Your image can impede you from being considered for new opportunities. Need a hint about the stuff you might reconsider posting?

- Overtly sexual content
- Hard-core cussing
- Racial, gender, religious slurs
- Intense and negative political anger

- Mind-altering activities

Look, supporting or sharing your opinion about something is fine. Consider leaving out the incensed baiting or provoking stuff.

And, for the self-employed entrepreneurs, don't think that you aren't being looked up. Haven't you done a quick search on your doctor, hair dresser, or the entrepreneur who you might be conducting business with?

Ask yourself: Do I stand by my post? How will this post come across? Is it worth posting? What is the point of this post? Would I consider me for a promotion if I were my boss? Would I hire me if I saw this post?

#boredatwork

Posting during work hours is one thing, but posting about how #bored you are, #leavingearly, #bossmanainthere, or a selfie at your desk eating a bowl of chili con carne! What are you thinking?

#boss on vacay; just #chilln.

"I have nothing to do." Really? I can see that stack of folders, dust all over the cabinet, and stuff all over your desk. (Selfie, remember?)

Wait for your break time to post and rant. Posting negative stuff about your job while on the job—does that make sense to you?

You're on a date, your date posts #frknbored, #outtahere… same principle. Disrespectful. Just sayin'.

New Ways to Gossip: Social Media

Gossip can ruin a reputation—yours and theirs. Avoid this teeny-bopper method of handling a conflict or dilemma.

Why would you expose yourself to the world as a gossiper? It's on record for eternity. Gossiping—especially during work hours or about coworkers—is unprofessional and it resolves nothing.

By the way, gossip is expressed in many ways, like posting quotes, images, or "posters" with messages to make your point about a certain someone, or openly exposing your issue; it will be crystal clear to everyone involved.

KEY POINTS:

- Be polite, attentive, and professional on the phone.
- Treat emails as if they are business letters, not tweets!
- Reply to emails and phone calls.
- Be mindful of what you post on social media— your reputation is on the line.
- There's nothing like a phone conversation or face-to-face meeting to really get to know someone.
- Don't gossip. Just don't.

CHAPTER 4

ALL THINGS BOSS

> "Nothing is as embarrassing as watching your boss do something you assured him couldn't be done." —Earl Wilson (American journalist and author)

Every boss is unique. The quicker you learn your boss's idiosyncrasies and preferences—and accept them—the quicker you will become the best darn employee (support partner) he or she has ever seen.

If she regularly comes in late, don't schedule any appointments until [insert time boss arrives] a.m.

If he likes to refill his travel mug when he arrives, make sure there is fresh-brewed coffee available.

If she likes her phone messages written down rather than emailed, write them down!

Complaining because she comes in late or you find it demeaning to have coffee ready for him will only show your boss that you are not the person that he or she can count on. And this, my friend, will only hinder your relationship and probability for a promotion or other fabulous merit increases.

Showing your boss that no job is too small or insignificant will (in most cases) be quickly noticed. Make yourself invaluable.

Although some of these topics are specific, the options are pretty generic and can be applied to similar situations.

> As with all of my opinions, advice, and options, consider them, consider your situation, consider your personal ethics, be discerning with advice from grouches, and consider company policies before taking action.
>
> Ultimately, it is your call. Ultimately, you have to live with your decision. Ultimately, it is your reputation.

THE BOSS'S
BLOW-UP

Your boss just blew up at you in front of a couple of coworkers. Do you stand up and go off on him? Do you get up and walk out? I wouldn't recommend it. You could:

A Return to your cubicle and immediately send an email to everyone you know explaining your side.

B   Listen to and acknowledge your boss's concern and quietly return to your duties.

C   Interrupt and insist that your boss hears you out while you list all of the wonderful things you've accomplished.

Answer: b. Clearly. It is very unprofessional for anyone to blow up at work. With that said, I've got to ask, did your boss have a valid reason to be ticked off at you? (Hold on, I'm not saying there is ever any reason for him or her to blow up.) If you did mess up, cool off, admit it, apologize, and fix it.

Before you blast off a "#bossisalunatic" on all of your social media platforms, go to your corner and stay there. This can help you avoid standing there totally embarrassed, hearing opinions and comments from coworkers, and most importantly, give you time to regain your composure.

Once you and your boss have had time to cool off, request an appointment to meet with him or her. Enter with a receptive attitude. Have a list prepared that includes just the facts.

Awkward or embarrassing moment at work? Acknowledge it. Offer a general apology to those around you. Something like, "Sorry that you all had to witness that," or "This was a tough lesson to learn." Return to your duties. No, you don't have to discuss it with everyone. Remember, how you handle a situation is more memorable than the actual situation. Do it with dignity.

Say your boss did not have a reason. He's just a jerk all of the time to everyone.

Options:

- Let it go; it was just your turn to be at the receiving end of today's wrath.
- Start looking for another job.
- Request a transfer to another department.
- Approach him or her and state your concerns. This could either prompt another unprofessional rant, get you on some "bad" list, bring awareness to his or her behavior, or put you in the unemployment line.
- Report it to HR.

Note: If your boss is a person of integrity, you will undoubtedly receive a sincere apology from him or her for the unprofessional delivery.

....

TROUBLE WITH THE BOSS?

You've decided that enough is enough; you aren't going to take it anymore! That was the last straw. Okay, I get your point.

After carefully thinking about it, you decide that you're going to march into his or her office and. . . . Hold on there, fireball!

Things to ask yourself before you request a meeting to hash things out with your boss:

- Will it really make a difference to him or her?

(Will it be dismissed, or will you really be heard?)

- Have others gone before me? Was the outcome a fiasco? (Yes? Maybe HR is the next step.)

- Is it merely a matter of principle? Is it worth fighting for?

- Am I going to be working here much longer? (Don't burn your bridge.)

- Have I asked for a lot of other things like time off, complained about coworkers, left early, had customer complaints, etc.?

- Is my boss the sole proprietor? (There's nowhere else to go if you aren't satisfied.)

With those points in mind, is it still worth requesting a meeting?

If the answer is yes, here is the next step:

- Approach your boss or his administrative assistant personally or via email to request a meeting (when they aren't busy, on the phone, already in a rotten mood, etc., . . . common sense required here).

- Be sure to have a positive attitude.

- Calm voice, please.

- Use polite words: please, thank you, I appreciate your time, I hope that you consider my request, etc.

- Do not tell your coworkers or customers about the meeting before you speak to your boss. (Chances are, your boss will have already heard about it—not a good way to go in.)

If your boss insists on talking about it right there and then in front of the world, suggest postponing it until your break or after you clock out. He or she may refuse, but you have the right to privacy.

Need to Change Your Schedule (or Have Another Special Request)?

Be specific and put some effort into your pitch.

Be prepared to explain why you want this change. (You like to sleep in? Probably won't be approved.)

Is the request temporary or permanent? A one-time thing or ongoing?

If your boss isn't open to your request, offer options. Ask him or her if they would consider the change on a trial basis; ask if you can try it for one month, then, at that time, you can meet again and discuss it.

What are you willing to do to show that you are flexible on other days? Tell your boss what you are willing to do. List the possible problems. (Your boss will see that you have given

More Things to Consider:

Keep in mind, as the boss, he or she has to get the job done—no matter what!

If you acknowledge the difficulty of their job, they may be more agreeable: "I know that you must receive a lot of requests and can't possibly agree to all of them. I understand. That is why I appreciate your time and consideration."

Imagine if they granted everyone's requests.

it some thought and that you are a team player by showing concern for the company and your coworkers.)

Be open to compromise. Your boss may not be able to agree to your "dream" schedule now, but he or she might be open to it two months from now. Are you willing to wait and accept these terms? Offer a couple of options. It isn't their job to fix it for you.

Wrong or right, sometimes the boss feels that he or she has to make a point. Your situation may be used as a lesson to the entire staff. No matter what, handle your boss's decision with a professional attitude. Don't flip out until you get home.

Mad? DO NOT:

- storm out
- slam doors
- throw stuff
- huff and puff
- roll your eyes

- gesture with any fingers
- mumble
- name-call or cuss
- spread the news
- threaten to quit

Finally, it may come down to deciding whether to stay and accept the terms or start looking for another job. Or, you might find that your services are no longer required.

If you don't get what you want, that's life. But no matter what, keep it together:

- Maintain a professional tone of voice.

- Manage your facial expressions.

- Do not gossip or complain to your coworkers.

- Maintain a positive attitude toward your customers and your boss. (You want a good recommendation, don't you?)

- Don't start slacking off or doing less than you normally do; in fact, do more. (You don't want to give your boss ANYTHING to use against you.)

And always keep in mind that no matter how awful the situation is, it is never permanent. Handle it with grace, respect, and a splash of humility—you'll feel better.

....

I CAUGHT MY BOSS . . .

From the Audience:

Q: I work in a warehouse for a midsize company. Once in a while, I need my boss's signature on a delivery receipt. He's usually on the floor, so I don't need to go to his office very often. This time I did. When I walked in, he was snorting cocaine with one of my coworkers. As soon as we made eye contact, I walked out. Within a couple of minutes, my boss came out to the floor and asked me what I needed; he signed the document and walked away. Neither one of us said anything. Now, I'm uncomfortable every time I see my coworker and my boss. Should I drop it, report them, or talk to them? I don't want to lose my job or get anyone in trouble.—Jonas

A: Dear Jonas,

If you talk to your boss about it, what is your point? Do

you want an explanation? What will you do with that information? What if he/she refuses to explain, or, even more awkward, denies it?

The same applies to your coworker. Do you know him/her well enough to bring it up privately, after work hours? What do you expect him/her to say; keep in mind, the boss is involved.

Options:

Discreetly give them both a schedule and list of locations of the nearest NA meetings. (Just kidding. Well, kinda.)

Explain that if you ever see this kind of behavior again, you will report them. (That's a bold, risky move; it's your word against theirs, and it may blacklist you for future promotions, etc.)

File a report with Human Resources. (Be prepared for battle).

Forget about it and try to reestablish your relationship. (It goes both ways.)

Manager Is Having an Affair

From the Audience:

Q: I accidently learned that my boss is having an affair with another dude. I don't want to be involved, but since he found out that I know, he's started talking to me about it . . . something that I'm really not cool with. I'm afraid if I shut him down it'll affect my raise, or I might even lose my job because of what I know. How do I get him to stop talking to me about it? —Todd

A: Dear Todd,

When you say "affair," I presume that one of the two love-birds is married—that's the only way to consider it an "affair." If they are both single, then that's just "dating."

I'm not sure what you aren't "cool" with—the affair or the gay relationship. Let's address it.

Gay relationships: You are free to approve or disapprove of whatever you want. That's the beauty of living in America. I also believe that sharing details of one's romantic relationship should not enter the workplace. Moving on . . .

> When you share personal information with a colleague, it can be detrimental to the relationship. How? Without asking them or considering it, you have decided to encumber them with your hanky-panky. It's like, "Hey, Laura, here's this huge box; just put it in your office somewhere and keep it there for me; and don't tell anyone about it."

Affairs in general: Many companies have a no-dating policy, generally between a manager and their subordinate. You can conclude why this is discouraged. Other companies have a notification policy where employees are required/encouraged to report when they've entered into a romantic relationship. Romantic relationships in the workplace can affect one's work and clarity of mind.

Options: Approach him and good naturedly and with all due respect tell him:

- "You know, Mr. Busy-Pants, I'm really glad that your personal life is so enjoyable, but I'm not into listening about other people's love lives."

- "I think it's against company policy, so you should be more discreet." (Kind of goody-two-shoes, but nice of you to point it out.)

- "Mr. Busy-Pants, it's cool that we have this camaraderie, but I'm of the "don't kiss and tell" philosophy." (Old school, he might appreciate that.)

- "Because of my personal or religious beliefs, this isn't something I like to discuss. I'm glad to know you're happy though."

Boss Exposed:

Catching your boss doing anything that would be considered inappropriate for the workplace is awkward, to say the least. How you handle the situation and yourself is of greater consequence.

1. Don't get dramatic!

2. If you must speak, keep your voice down.

3. Walk away, giving everyone involved time to compose themselves.

4. Do not blab, post on social media, email, text, or use any other form of communication to tell anyone about the incident.

5. Allow your boss to make the first move (this might take a few days).

6. Resume your duties immediately.

7. If you meet with your boss to discuss the incident, maintain confidentiality.

Common sense dictates that you skip the above steps if the incident puts anyone in danger or is potentially detrimental or corrupt.

....

LAST MINUTE PROJECTS, LAST MINUTE REQUESTS

You're sending off a text to your friends, "On my way!" As you check your email one last time before logging off, a new one appears, and it's from your manager. In the subject line, you read: "On my way down."

Your entire body stiffens, and you think, *Can I get outta here before he . . .* Too late! You hear footsteps approaching. "Got a minute?" says your manager.

You let out a breath and take in another; trying to sound upbeat, you guardedly reply, "I was just on my way out, but sure."

He sits down and hands you a fistful of papers. "Do these make any sense to you?"

One hour and eleven text alerts later, your manager asks you to stay and finish up what you've started together.

What would you do? Multiple Choice.

A   Stand your ground and tell him that you've got plans and have people waiting for you.

B   Inform him that you have only a few minutes, listen to his concerns, and tell him that you'll come in extra early tomorrow and work on it then.

C   Stay as long as he needs you to stay.

D   Stay, but subtly let him know that you're not happy about it.

E "Excuse me for a moment, Mr. Manager, while I quickly let my friends know that I'll be delayed a bit." (Hope he gets it and keeps you only a few minutes.)

> "Most bosses know instinctively that their power depends more on an employee's compliance than on threats or sanctions."—Fernando Bartolme, Professor of Management, Instituto de Empresa

There are so many variables to consider when you make this decision.

- Are you working toward a promotion?
- Is this an opportunity to have personal contact with your manager?
- Is this an opportunity to show your manager that he can count on you?
- Is one of many dinners with friends really more significant than private time with your manager?
- Is this a recurring practice?
- Are the "fistful of papers" things he dumps on you and then takes credit for himself?
- Are you new to the company?
- Of course, if your impending date is significant, like celebrating an anniversary or birthday, have prepurchased tickets, you're taking off for the weekend, caring for a sick family member, a salon appointment, or catching the last train out, speak up!

If you decide to stay, don't whine and complain about it to your coworkers the next day. That's just tacky, and you'll lose all the benefits and brownie points you gained by staying.

Answers. If you picked:

A Go ahead, but you may lose his respect. If you choose this route, be sure that you say it in an apologetic and respectful manner.

B He may or may not take only a few minutes. You will have to be prepared to end the conversation and come in earlier as promised.

C This is usually the best option.

D Oh, he'll get the message and learn that you are a whiny pouter. Either do it gladly or don't agree to it.

E There's always a chance.

I Am Not a Wedding Planner!

"The trouble with doing something right the first time is that nobody appreciates how difficult it was."–Walter J. West, American football player (but probably an admin.)

From the Audience:

Q: My boss is getting married. His fiancée is working out of the country, so a large part of the research, planning, and follow-up is falling on his lap, and now on mine.

In addition to my regular duties, I cover for absent admins, leaving me behind on my work. Adding "wedding planner" duties is preposterous!

I'm receiving calls from caterers, bands, and other wedding-related people—and they're asking for me! I'm constantly in and out of his office, and I just can't take it anymore. How do I resign as his wedding planner?—Sophia

A: Dear Sophia,

Before you get to a boiling point, schedule a meeting with him. And do not discuss this or complain to anyone in the building. Conducting personal business on company time is unethical. Oh, a phone call or two—we've all done it. But this sounds like hours are being devoted to the upcoming nuptials.

Consider this:

- He trusts you with his personal affairs. (Don't blow this! Maintain confidentiality; gossiping is prohibited.)
- He trusts your taste and judgment. (But of course.)
- He knows you can "do it all." (Well, naturally.)
- Is he acknowledging and compensating you for doing this exclusive work? (It doesn't help you get your day-to-day duties done, but it's something.)
- Is his fiancée under the impression that he's doing it all? (That could get awkward when he gets caught.)
- Does your relationship have a personal component? (That might give him the impression that you are "friends" and that you'd be willing to handle this kind of work for him.)

- Are you invited to the wedding? (Not that you'd want to attend, but if you planned it . . .)

At the meeting: Don't get dramatic. Don't start verbally dancing around with oodles of examples to explain why you can't be his wedding planner. Keep it plain and simple.

- "I appreciate the trust and confidence you have in me, but . . . "
- Begin with the obvious. "I am not a wedding planner."
- "I don't have experience to make these decisions."
- "These extra responsibilities are affecting my workload." (I recommend this one; he can't argue with it.)
- "Here is a list of reputable wedding consultants." (Obviously, prepare in advance.)

....

OUT IN THE FIELD
WITH MY BOSS

Does your boss engage in shady activities when he's out in field?

- Opening up a brewski while driving?
- Taking a little siesta at lunch, waking up just in time for the afternoon break?
- Popping into a "gentlemen's club" for lunch?
- Spending way too much time playing games on her tablet?

- Running a couple of errands during work hours?
- Spilling his guts about his rotten love life or sharing lewd commentary about coworkers?

Weird, right? To say the least, awkward. Do you report him? Do you warn her? Do you ignore it? Do you join him?

Let's take one at a time.

And he's always lecturing *us* about teamwork . . . Lucky he's got that hard hat on.

Do you report him?

"Yes": He may get fired; he may find a way to fire you or make your life miserable; he could implicate you; he could learn from his ninety-day suspension and become a changed man.

"No": He may get caught anyway. You would have to prove that although present, you did not participate. An accident may occur if you knowingly allowed him to drink and drive. You have placed yourself in a potentially detrimental situation—that's not good for your career.

Do you warn her?

"Yes": Maybe she needs a wake-up call. Maybe she'll transfer you. She can ignore the warning, though, so protect yourself. (Make a note somewhere of your conversation.)

"No": Nothing will change. Business as usual.

Do you ignore it?

This is the most uncomplicated and painless strategy. Keep in mind that you might be found guilty by association. If this was a one- or two-time incident, perhaps this would be the way to go.

Do you join him?

Please don't. But that's your call.

If none of the above options suit you, request a transfer, look for a new job, or speak to your HR department using the transparent phrase, "I have this friend . . ."

....

"YOU'RE WELCOME . . ." HELLOOO!

I've been asked a time or two: "How can I get my boss to say "Please" and "Thank you" to me?"

Well, the next time he or she asks you to do something, you can reply, "What's the magic word?" (tempting, but I don't recommend it). Your boss might get it and shamefully or reluctantly say it, walk away thinking *That was weird*, or confront you with a terse, "Excuse me?"

If it is that important to you, as with most situations, talk it out. This one, I must admit, might be a little awkward. "Uh, ma'am, I would like you to use your 'Magic Words' when you speak to me."

Casually mention to your boss that you have been reading this etiquette book about "workplace dilemmas" and that the number one complaint is that people don't say "Please" and "Thank you" enough.

This seems like a good place to share my "Every Day Words" list:

My Every Day Words

"Please"
Use: When you ask for anything! This includes directions and assistance (verbal or physical).

"Thank you"
Use: When you receive anything! A compliment, directions, a gift, help, etc.

"You're welcome"
Use: After someone says "Thank you." Please stop saying, "No problem." (Whew! I didn't realize that I could have been "a problem.")

"Pardon me" (kind of like asking for forgiveness)
Use: After an accidental burp or passing gas. When you need to pass/get through.

"Excuse me" (kind of like requesting permission)
Use: Before pushing your way through a crowded elevator.
When you need to leave. To interrupt (if you must).

"I'm sorry"
Use: If you've insulted someone (intentionally or otherwise).
If you didn't keep your word. If you've flipped-out. If you've
caused anguish, pain, or disappointment to anyone. If you
forgot to reply to an email or phone message. This phrase,
said with sincerity, can resolve—or, at the very least, minimize—the intensity of the situation.

*Warning: Frequent use of these words may result in more
pleasant interactions and work atmosphere.*

....

HOLIDAY PARTY HIJACK

You invite your staff of five to your home for a holiday get-to-
gether as a way of thanking them for another great year. It's
all set, they can all make it, and the caterer has confirmed.

But wait, your boss learns about your shindig (old school
for "party") and proceeds to ramble off names of employees
that he's in charge of. "Let them know about it," he proclaims.
"And be sure you include their families . . . by the way, what
are you serving?"

Before you can think and flat-out reject his intrusion, you
hear yourself listing the menu. And that is where he crosses
the line (for the second or third time!). "I don't think anyone's

gonna like the scampi, especially the kids." Wha'! Kids? And you realize that your party has been hijacked!

Hijacked is hijacked. It doesn't matter whether it's a party, a project, your lunch plans, a meeting, your wedding, etc. Piggybacking on someone's existing thing is uncool, unprofessional, unpardonable, underhanded, and unthinking, and it makes you a pitiful freeloader. Did I cover it?

Options? If you don't speak up right there and then, it will become even harder to unravel once the word spreads. Let's say you froze, and your boss has just emailed you his list along with menu recommendations (which are really orders).

Request to meet privately, ASAP!

Without providing too many reasons (scamps like these will find a way to "fix it" or get around it), you can begin with:

"I **cannot** (key word) entertain a large group. Perhaps we can consider combining our parties next year."

What would you do? He starts tossing his credit card or cash, telling you, "If it's the money, I got it covered."

Next step: Repeat. "I'm sorry, I am not in a position to entertain a large group." (Yep, it's the same, but repetition is key. If you deviate, you'll open the door to an unending bout of wheeling-and-dealing.) Then get up and walk out. If the word has already spread, send out an email apologizing for the "misunderstanding," wrapping it up by wishing everyone a wonderful holiday. If you'd like to rub salt in the wound (another old-school term), you may add, "If you have any questions, please see [insert your boss's name]."

This method can be applied to any cunning party crasher.

·····················

THE BOSS'S KID

From the Audience:

Q: I work in the warehouse of a pretty big company. About a month ago, my supervisor told me I had to train the daughter of one of the big executives. She's working here for the summer. The kid has been a real pain. I can't get my job done because I'm babysitting her and fixing everything she messes up. After I explain it for the third and fourth time, she grunts and just doesn't seem to care. She's always checking her cell phone (they aren't allowed when you're on the floor) and takes longer breaks than she's supposed to. I've had it! How can I handle this without losing my job or having this kid report me to her daddy? —Alexander

Daddy's little lass is a pain in my . . . ahem.

A: Dear Alexander,

Having anyone from the boss's family work for you is seldom a blessing and often complex. If the infractions are safety related, report it right away.

I recommend that you document excessive breaks, cell phone use, and blunders. Formally remind Daddy's little miss of the company rules, wait for a nod of acknowledgment, and document it. With document in hand, speak to your immediate supervisor. He or she will take it from there—maybe nowhere, but you've done your duty and covered your gluteus maximus.

All you can do now is to continue documenting and count down the days until school starts up again.

....

"FRIENDING" YOUR BOSS

From the Audience:

Q: My boss and me are cool with each other, can I "friend" her?"—Kyle

A: Dear Kyle,

Don't . . . unless it is a professional site. "Cool" with each other at work does not mean that she wants to be cool *witchu* outside work. It's a good idea to check the company policy before you send the request. Maybe check to see if she is friends with any other employees. Personally, I'd leave it up to your boss to make the first move.

Q: My boss sent me a "friend" request. I don't want to accept it. What should I do?—Kristen

A: Dear Kristen,

Presuming this is on your "personal" social media page, leave it hanging. Unless they're sitting there waiting for the "accept" notification, they probably will never know.

If they ask you about it (rude and awkward), reply with something like, "I'm so bad at checking my notifications." Or "You aren't the first one to remind me; I just never get to them," and change the subject quickly.

Take the open and honest route, and tell them that while you appreciate the "invitation," you've learned from your parents/professor/older brother's experience that keeping one's personal and professional lives separate has proven to be the preferred choice . . . "I just want to make sure you don't get the wrong impression. . . . My friends would probably feel kind of uncomfortable knowing I'm connected with my boss."

....

FLYING ON THE JOB

If you are travelling with your boss or person of higher rank, be attentive and defer to them. Don't start acting or speaking in a laid-back and chummy manner just because you're not "in the office." (Take the cue from your boss.)

Allow them to take the better seat, and let them dictate whether they feel like talking. (Watch for clues: reading, earphones, eyes closed, or looking out the window probably means your boss doesn't want to chat.)

Be wise when talking about yourself, your accomplishments, or your ideas. Throw it out there; if he or she responds, go with it. Keep it brief and relevant, and avoid trite details.

Be available if he or she wants to discuss something. (If you doze off, be sure not to nuzzle up against the boss.)

Eat before you board (unless it's a thirteen-hour flight or the meal is included).

Try not to drink alcohol (one with a meal, maybe). Show your boss you're capable and ready for business.

Respectfully speak to the flight attendants. (Please don't be that demanding passenger everyone dreads.)

And most importantly, you are not at home in the privacy of your living room. (Keep your shoes on, belt buckled, and hopefully your skirt isn't slipping up.)

KEY POINTS:

- Your boss is your superior in the workplace—maintain boundaries and be respectful!
- Avoid getting too personal, too casual, or too cocky with your boss.
- Consider carefully before you approach your boss with complaints, accusations, or recommendations.
- When in doubt on how to, or whether to, approach your boss, seek advice from a discreet and well-respected colleague or HR.

CHAPTER 5

MEETINGS, NETWORKING, AND TRADE SHOWS

If it's work related, it should be work behavior. Depending on the type of industry, who's in attendance, or purpose of the meeting, a more relaxed frame of mind might be copacetic.

This also applies to a networking function. No matter how laid-back the vibe is, maintain at least a splash of professionalism.

....

ATTENDING THE MEETING

It is irrelevant whether you believe that meetings are a waste of time or not.

Attend every meeting with a good attitude. Take it seriously even when others don't. Keep in mind that some meetings are recorded. Don't be caught dozing off or rolling your eyes. Minimize the things you do that might distract others.

Perception: *Man, what a bore; there are a million other places I'd like to be.*

Here are fifteen "Concentration Killers":

1   A ringing (or vibrating) cell phone.

2   Glancing down to identify the incoming text, call, social media posts, notifications, etc.

3   Constantly checking the time (especially if it's on your phone).

4   Chewing gum.

5   Walking out during a presentation (especially if you have to walk directly in front of speaker).

6   Walking in during a presentation (Be on time!).

7   Making constant trips to the refreshment table.

8   Digging through your handbag.

9   Eating—crinkling your wrapper, licking your fingers, or smacking and chomping with your mouth open.

10   Clicking your pen.

11   Constant "sighing" or openly yawning.

12   Making constant commentary.

13   Constantly interrupting to "clarify" or show off how much you think you know.

14   Flipping pages.

15   Fidgeting with your hair, picking your teeth, chewing your nails, using your key to clean under your nails, or digging for ear wax.

The Sprawling Attendee

You arrive early to select the perfect seat, the one where you can see the presenter without any obstructions and where you will be undetected should you need to excuse yourself—perfect. You settle in and mark your territory with the water-filled Styrofoam cup.

Feeling secure about reserving the perfect seat, you proceed to mix and mingle with the other attendees before the presentation begins.

A bell rings, signaling that it is time to take your seat. Only a few stop their conversation and meander to their pre-established seats, while others continue their ever-so-compelling conversation, standing in the way and forcing the organizer to once again ring the bell.

The presentation begins. Most attendees pull out a pen to jot down notes or doodle on the handout. Next to you, the tech-savvy person pulls out her tablet. She first adjusts her chair; moving it back and at an angle, she imposes herself into your space. Naturally, the cell phone takes its prominent place on the table, the cup of water must now be moved over, and of course the handouts must be visible. Where does that leave you, the poor under-teched attendee? If the incessant shaking of her foot wasn't enough of a distraction, the sprawling of her essential belongings all over your table space is enough to drive you away.

By the way, this actually happened to me. I could have looked at her and said something like, "They sure don't give us much space do they?" and hope that she would get it and move her stuff over.

Tech gadgets are very useful. I embrace them—well, I am trying to—but the point is that no matter what you decide to use to take notes, be mindful of space and sound. If you choose to use a device that emits any sound, sit in the back. Sprawlers must reel in their material; it comes down to consideration—not only to those around you, but also to the speaker. Candy wrappers, a jingling mint tin, an ever-so-quick whisper, the sound of texting, rummaging through your bag, or any other minor action is a distraction and is discourteous.

Another option: "Excuse me, please. I don't want to knock over your water." Even though I was there first (playground rules apparently did not apply here), at the break, I gathered my cup and moved.

Dear Sprawler,

Before you arrange your stuff and make yourself comfortable at the next conference or training workshop, keep in mind that someone is watching and forming an opinion about you. Namely, the person next to you. You could lose the interest of a potential client, employer, or collaborating partner, or simply be embarrassed by someone who just happens to tell it like it is.

The Primping Ponytailer

We've all experienced the tightly-fitted seating arrangements at workshops or conferences when you reluctantly have to ask the person next to you to get up so that you can excuse yourself.

> Tightly-squeezed? Consider this: make an effort to use the restroom, refresh your coffee cup, make your calls, etc., at the same time the people next to you do.

And then you have the odd irritant.

Sitting directly in front of me was a gentleman who continuously, almost habitually, undid and redid his ponytail throughout the entire presentation. Was it nerves, limp rubber in the rubber band, he loved his hair, or was he seeking a compliment about his golden locks? Whatever the case, it was most distracting.

This is specifically for people (men and women) with long hair. Reasons you don't redo your "do":

- Don't redo your ponytail with arms extended, so that if your neighbor were to turn their head to one side, their face would be in your arm pit, or an elbow, upside their head.

- Don't redo your ponytail; some of your precious strands will inevitably land on your neighbor.

- Don't redo your ponytail; you block the view of the person(s) behind you.

- Don't redo your ponytail; personal grooming should be done in private.

Consider this: If your hair requires constant attention, find a new hairstyle!

How to Make the Crinkling Stop?

You just can't take the crinkling, clicking, or smacking anymore, so you take the first step: you overemphasize adjusting your sitting position (sometimes accompanied by a sigh), clearly the universal message for, "Your crinkling is bugging me; please stop it." Message not received. And every time he or she goes in to take his or her next bite, the crinkling seems to become louder.

I believe that most people are unaware of the "deafening" and sometimes disgusting sounds they are making. Certainly there are times that a polite request can help resolve a situation. Most people are embarrassed and are usually quite happy to accommodate a request. If not, at the next break, move.

Your Feet

In certain parts of the country, flip-flops are now considered business-appropriate footwear. Okay, whatever (in some fields it might be fine); however, if you are rubbing your foot, massaging a toe, and picking under the toenail, I have a problem (most people would).

Do flip-flops really give you the professional look you want the boss to see? Oh, the boss wears flip-flops to work? Cool, just don't play with your feet. I might have to shake your hand or be the recipient of the bottle of water you are kindly handing me. Foot hand—yuck!

Rosalinda Gets Personal:

Sitting at a meeting, the man next to me takes his left leg and pulls it up placing it on his right knee. Great, now his nasty foot is right next to me. If that's not enough to gross you out—he begins rubbing up and down his leg. Just a habit, you say?

Instinctively, his fingers made their way down to his toes. He fiddled around . . . I couldn't watch. Then I hear FTP (fidgety toe picking). Looking across the room, I saw another person who had succumbed to FTP.

Please keep your hands away from your feet—you are not in the privacy of your own home. And by the way, please keep your foot away from me!

You're Late!

It's distracting when someone walks in while the meeting

is in progress. Sometimes it can't be helped, but if it is always the same person, we begin to resent them, roll our eyes, glance over at the person across the table with an "of course" expression, and we may even conclude that the latecomer must think that they're better than everyone else.

If you are the late person, that may be what people are thinking about you; plan ahead and be on time. Find a seat near you and don't roam around the room looking for your friend.

Leaving Early?

Don't. If you must, make it a rare occurrence and for business reasons. Be sure to arrive a few minutes early to apologize and inform the speaker/host of your early departure. Wait for a pause or transitioning moment to slip out. Sit near the door so you can easily and quietly slip out.

You're Accused

There you are, doodling on your notepad when you hear a colleague mention your name—and not in an endearing tone. She points to you, accusing you as the problem, but none of it is true. (Remember, you are trying to build a professional reputation, which requires a calm and civil demeanor.)

If this topic is on the agenda, you can certainly address it. Briefly. You might recommend that you meet privately after the meeting.

If things get heated in the boardroom, open a window. (Wink, wink.) Seriously, if you think you're going lose it, excuse yourself. Don't speak to anyone. Sometimes that can just fuel the fire. Take a walk or go to another floor. Do whatever you have to do to be alone—even if that means sitting in a bathroom stall. Later, apologize to the host of the meeting.

> "Speak when you are angry and you will make the best speech you will ever regret."—Ambrose Bierce, American journalist and satirist

You Arrive on Time but No One Is There!

The appointment was scheduled one week ago and confirmed this morning. You arrive to find the office lights off. You stand by for several minutes. You return to the receptionist to inquire about any messages that might be there for you. Thirty minutes later, you leave.

Sudden illness, car trouble, or unexpected traffic delays are a few reasons beyond our control. However, forgetfulness is not.

Of course, he's late again! P.S. Fashion note: a tie should be worn a bit longer.

Of course, it has happened to everyone, or if it hasn't, it will eventually. With so many forms of communication, though, we expect an attempt to make contact.

How long do you wait for a person to arrive before you leave? Some say between fifteen minutes a half hour.

If you are at a restaurant, you can leave a message with the host; at the office, you can leave a message with an administrative professional.

You decide:

He/She stood me up . . .

He should make the first move and contact me.

I'll contact her requesting that we reschedule.

That's it! I don't do business with no-shows.

He'd better have a good reason or else I'm done.

I'll give it a day or two and see what happens.

Your response may vary depending on the familiarity of the relationship, or how badly you want this client or job.

If the no-show holds a significant position, allow them at least several hours to make the first move. If you do not hear from them, send a brief note: "I'm sorry we weren't able to meet today. I am still interested in meeting with you. If your schedule allows, we can meet at the same place on . . . " Depending on your relationship, you might add a brief phrase of concern like, I hope everything is all right.

The Latecomer from Another Land

From the Audience:

Q: How many times do you put up with someone who is

always late? Not five or ten minutes, but thirty to forty-five minutes late. I recently brought it to his attention, and he justified himself by telling me that, in his culture, time wasn't concrete, and followed that with, "You need to learn how to relax." He has been in the US for years!—Joshua

A: Dear Joshua,

Is this a client, coworker, or boss? Let's take it one by one:

A Client: Simple. How badly to do you need or want this account? Is it worth all the time you waste waiting?

A Coworker: Easy. Schedule the meeting in-house. That way, if he isn't where he's supposed to be, you can leave a note and return to your desk—he'll eventually show up.

A Boss: If it's your boss who insists on meeting off-site, take a good book with you, catch up on emails, and wait. Suggest holding your meetings in-house or offer to drive together to the off-site location.

No matter who it is, you can take the direct route and explain that you have a tight schedule and even a few minutes can take you off track. You can throw in a diplomatic line: "Your country's attitude about time sounds very relaxing, but unfortunately, it isn't that way here." Ask him to call next time if he is running late. Remember, tact is essential—especially if you are dealing with your boss.

The Forgotten Appointment

What can you do when you're the flake?

- Call them as soon as possible. (Unless you can't even remember you had a meeting.)

Rosalinda Gets Personal:

Recently, I forgot to show up for an appointment. My reason? I didn't check my calendar. I know that on Tuesdays I don't start teaching until noon—so why would I look? Because I made a morning appointment, that's why. What a surprise when I answered my phone and heard, "Hello, this is Madison . . . didn't we have an appointment this morning?"

- If they don't answer, don't get dramatic and jump to conclusions that they don't like you anymore. Leave a brief message, stating that you will try again later. (It was your mess-up; you call back.)

- Apologize twice. Once at the beginning of the conversation and once in closing. What are you apologizing for? Wasting their time, that's what! Don't go on and on about how sorry you are—it'll start to sound disingenuous.

- Keep your list of excuses to one or none. Add that you were looking forward to meeting with them.

- When you reschedule, make sure that it is at the other person's convenience.

- Be sure to pick up the coffee tab. (It's a nice gesture after wasting their time. And please don't say things like "I owe you . . . this will make up for . . . " Are you saying that their time is only worth a cup of coffee? Just do it.)

- Consider sending a brief email the day before to confirm the new appointment. That will give the

person you are meeting peace of mind and as-
sure them that your forgetfulness is not a habit.

- Move on. Don't bring it up. And if they do, deal
with it as professionally and as graciously as
possible.

Your Grand Entrance: "Wassup?"

Making connections can happen anywhere. So why do some
people appear so unprepared when they attend a business-related function?

A first impression takes only moments to make, but a
long and gradual process to undo. Below are a few practices
to consider when you attend a meeting or networking event:

Your Grand Entrance: Entering as though you are the
main attraction is a no-no. So is swaggering in with your
hands in your pockets, giving everyone a nod as you greet
them with a "Wassup?"—save it for a social occasion. However, slithering in without making eye contact and tucking
yourself into a corner is equally unprofessional.

Appearance: Shower, people! (Meeting with me in your
sticky-sweaty t-shirt after spin class won't make me wanna
sit too close to you.) Comb your hair! Wear something professional and clean. Your comfy football-logo PJ bottoms are
not appropriate. Nor is your faded, worn-out, embellished
penguins-holding-balloons sweatshirt (unless you sell embellished sweatshirts).

I Hear You: Loud sighs of boredom, grunts of disapprov-
al, whispered comments to whomever will listen to you, and

the opening and closing of your notebook are all unprofessional gestures. If you're bored, excuse yourself and go home.

Consider this: Maintaining a professional appearance will enhance your credibility. If you aren't sure about your current look, seek assistance from a professional image consultant—the investment is worth it.

P.S. Do not pass out your business card as though you were a Vegas card dealer. Talk to the person; if they're interested, they'll ask for it. (By the way, when you hand out your card, hand it with the info facing up, toward the person, make sure it isn't sticky or stained, and please be sure the information is current.)

....

HOSTING THE MEETING

When you are hosting a meeting, always follow proper protocol. If you don't, why should they? And if there isn't a method in place, start one. People will take your lead.

Arrive on time! Begin on time! End on time! With this formula, your staff will be more inclined to attend obligingly. This shows that you are respectful of their time.

> "A meeting is an event at which the minutes are kept and the hours are lost."—Unknown

A few more tips to make meetings a little more tolerable and build rapport and trust:

- Allow for a break every hour to ninety minutes or so. If you're close to concluding, tell them.
- Be prepared.
- Stick to the agenda. (It'll help keep the meeting on track.)
- Master how to shut down the chatterbox. (There's always one in the crowd.)
- Be clear about Q&A; will it be throughout or at the end? (If it's at the end, and you take some throughout, you might lose control of your audience and/or believability.)
- Don't use the floor to talk about your new puppy, your upcoming surgery, or any other personal stuff.
- Providing refreshments or raffling off a coffee gift card can't hurt.
- If time allows, pass out a few compliments for work well done.

"Hold on." (Is there anything wrong with this picture?)

You're Hosting a Meeting in Your Office?

You're obviously expecting someone; you made the appointment to meet, right? Out of respect for them, you should be prepared. Acting startled when they show up on time is kind of lame and unprofessional. "Oh, is it that time already?" Also:

- Clean up a bit. At least clear off the guest chair and a little spot for their water bottle.
- Take care of your bathroom business before they arrive.
- Minimize the screen on your computer. Try to shut off the slide show; this is distracting to your guest.
- Mute your phone. Let it go to voicemail.
- If the topic of conversation is personal or of a sensitive nature, close your office door. Oh, no door? Perhaps you should use a conference room.
- Stand up and shake your visitor's hand. You may skip the handshake if you see them all the time.
- If you bring your pooch to work, keep in mind that your office may have a certain scent that might be a little whiffy to others. (A little lavender spritz might be nice.) Also, Fido can detract from the conversation. Conference room?

Q: When I receive a female visitor in my office, I should:

A say nothing and let her sit where she wishes.

B gesture and tell her where to sit.

C say, "Please, sit wherever you'd like."

A: And the answer is . . . b. Are you surprised? If you have only one chair aside from your plush ergonomic leather desk chair, she will no doubt make the right decision and take the metal frame chair next to the garbage can. Even though there is an obvious choice, it's still nice to gesture to tell your guest to "Please, take a seat."

By the way, it doesn't matter whether your guest is male or female; I just threw it in for fun.

If you're a guest, technically, you should not take your seat until you are asked to do so by the office host.

Can We Meet Later?

What can you do when someone can't allow you into his or her office for your scheduled meeting? It might be overlooked if the reason is beyond the person's control, like there is a rat infestation, spilled pickle juice that just reeks, or a feng shui practitioner is busy giving the office a final touch.

But when the reason is within his or her control—a colleague is using the office phone, his puppy is asleep, or her out-of-town cousin is changing—this can be irksome.

This is when I wish we'd bring back a little formality to the workplace. While things do come up, personal stuff should rarely conflict with professional stuff.

Options:

- You can reschedule.
- You can explain to him or her that your time is valuable, etc. (This option is probably not worth it; you'll get an apology, but it won't change

anything.)

- You can take the meeting to another location. (Oh wait, he can't because he has to keep an eye on the sleeping puppy or the feng shui praction- er might have a question.)

- You can hold your meeting just outside the of- fice, making sure you keep your voice down.

- You can get to the point and cut the meeting short.

- Or you can walk away frustrated.

A meeting is a time to build a relationship with a cowork- er, boss, or client. The lack of preparedness could damage your professional reputation or be to blame for the loss of a client.

....

THE COMPANY PARTY

The threat of a "video gone viral" should not be the main reason to deter you from misbehaving at the company party.

> "You moon the wrong person at an office party and suddenly you're not professional anymore."—Jeff Foxworthy, American comedian and author

I'm not saying that you can't let your hair down a bit. Go ahead and share a few details about your personal life, but keep it family-friendly and professional.

If you think company parties are a bore, think of them as an extension of your job.

Consider these top nine niceties:

1 Smile. Choose to have a positive attitude. (People will notice.)

2 Don't bring along an uninvited guest.

3 Don't flirt. Or at least be sure it isn't the boss's wife or husband.

4 You are there to mingle. (Sitting in a corner or hanging out with only your department? Why bother coming to the party?)

5 Keep your cell phone in your pocket.

6 "Open bar" doesn't mean "all you can drink"!

7 Don't moan about lack of raise, limited benefits, or any other unpleasant work topics.

8 Greet and thank the host(s).

9 If you've got your nightclub or dive bar clothes on because that's where you're headed after this dull office party, keep your coat on.

....

NETWORKING

From Shy to Charming

From the Audience:

Q: I recently lost my job of seven years. I've had a few interviews, but no job offers. A few of my friends are encouraging me to go to networking events with them. I'm hesitant to attend because I am embarrassed to tell anyone that I'm un-employed. To make things worse, I'm not a very outgoing person. Any tips? — Reuben

A: Dear Reuben,

If you believe that you have a shy nature, it is only natural to be hesitant about meeting new people. Just remember that many of the people at networking events are in the same position.

14 Tips For "Observers" (And Novices):

Being an introvert is not a permanent state of mind. Besides, in my humble opinion, an introvert is an "observer." Not everyone dives in. Observers need a little time to survey the situation, evaluate, and then react accordingly.

First, proudly acknowledge the fact that you decided to attend a networking event. And secondly, know that you are not the only one there that is uncomfortable.

Here are fourteen things that you can do to ease into networking.

Consider these tips:

1 Attend with a seasoned networking buddy. (He/she can make the introductions. Don't latch on to them throughout the event though.)

2 Wear something you feel good in. (There's nothing like an uncomfortable, ill-fitting outfit to wipe out your confidence.)

3 Do a little research about the networking event, or contact the organizer in advance. Ask

whatever questions you have: how many people are expected, who are most repeat attendees, will there be a speaker. . . . Most organizers are happy to provide information.

4   Starting a conversation is probably the most paralyzing part of networking. Look up some fun and random events/people that are #trending online. Introducing a light-hearted subject will put everyone at ease, which in most cases, encourages conversation, making it easier for you. (*"Today I read about . . ."*)

5   Set a comfortable time limit, even if it is only thirty minutes. (No matter how it goes, you'll find comfort knowing that you are leaving soon. It's *your* time limit; you can always extend it.)

6   Drive your own car. (You'll have peace of mind knowing that you aren't stuck.)

7   Stop in the restroom first. (One step at a time.) Wash your hands. Make sure everything is zipped up, take a squirt of breath freshener, and take a deep breath.

8   Approach a group of two or three. If they are in the middle of the "what do you dos," smile and listen until it is your turn.

9   Avoid approaching a solitary person. Two "observers" in one group is one too many. (You can invite him/her to walk over to a group with you. If you can do that, you are no longer an introvert!)

10 If you don't know what to do with your hands,

carry a portfolio. Besides it gives you a place to keep all of the business cards you'll be receiving.

11   Don't worry about forgetting someone's name. Politely, ask them to repeat it. Even the most experienced networkers forget. That's why we wear name badges. (Place name badge on upper right shoulder for easy reference.)

12   Don't hesitate to excuse yourself if there is unbearable silence, especially if you've done "your part." Simply say something like, "I think I'll go mingle. Would you please excuse me." Or "Well, it was nice chatting with you; I'm sure we'll run into each other again. Enjoy the evening."

13   Not all networking groups are the same. Unfortunately, some are cliquish and even unfriendly. Try to not take it personally.

14   Consider joining a speaking group, find a mentor, hang around positive outgoing people, take an improv class (I've recently done this; you'll gain confidence while having fun), take a class that requires engaging in conversation with others, volunteer...being involved in extracurricular activities will expose you to new things, hence giving you more to talk about.

Fifteen Networking Etiquette Truisms: It Makes Sense to Me

1   Practice your handshake.

Consider this:

Whom are you drawn to? Someone who seems pleasant, interested in others, and is standing tall? Focus on those traits. Don't forget to smile. "There is no personal charm so great as the charm of a cheerful temperament."—Henry Van Dyke (American author, educator, and clergyman)

2 Don't call me by a nickname—especially if we've just met.

3 If you wear a low-cut blouse, right or wrong, expect them to look.

4 If your hands are in your pockets, I probably won't approach you. (Keep your hands to your sides. Carry a portfolio; it'll help you with AHC, "awkward hand complex.")

5 If you introduce yourself, hand me your business card, and then immediately excuse yourself to get a plate of appetizers, don't expect your card to make it into my Rolodex.

6 If your hands are full with a filled-to-the-rim glass of free wine and a plate piled high with free treats, I probably won't approach you.

Eating: If you must snack during a workshop or while networking, please don't lick your fingers—we may be shaking hands later. And close your mouth when you chew, pretty please. Thank you.

7   If I express interest in you, but not in your product, and you take offense, I probably won't be referring you to anyone.

8   Please take small bites; I don't enjoy seeing your bulging cheek while you are trying to sell me something.

9   Don't divulge your entire personal life to me.

10   Don't play the "desperate" role.

11   Attend with a pleasant disposition. Smile.

12   If you couldn't take time to shower . . . need I say more?

13   Turn the ringer off and stay off your mobile phone.

14   Look at me when we're talking.

15   Don't get offended when I politely try to end your thirty-seven-minute sales pitch.

Rosalinda Gets Personal:

One of my most unappetizing experiences was speaking with a woman who was munching away at the freebie appetizers. She was commenting on how people really needed etiquette these days. Smiling (thankfully with closed lips), I felt a dewy morsel from her last opened-mouth chew land on my lip. (Are you close to vomiting yet?) She was oblivious to it. What did I do? The first moment she looked down at her plate, I took my hand as discreetly as possible and wiped the wet sticky morsel away with my hand, trying hard not to involuntarily lick my lips. Shortly after that, I excused myself; heading straight to the restroom, I dabbed a little water on my lip and reapplied my lipstick. This is one of a few reasons I rarely eat at networking events, and am inclined to evade talking with people who are shoveling food into their mouths.

More on Networking

Consider this:

- Have business cards printed; include your name (no nicknames) and contact information.
- Dress as if you care.
- Be prepared to briefly explain what you are looking for. Please don't say, "Anything!" How is that helpful to anyone?

- Don't go straight for the food and drink. (What is your purpose in being there?)

- Please leave your darling pooch, Apollina, at home. (You won't be able to focus entirely on the person or event.)

- Approach anyone who is standing alone. Chances are they are getting their feet wet.

- Ask people questions about their interests, how they got into their industry, or start with the weather. Yes, the weather. You'd be surprised how the conversation can take off. Of course, you must be a little creative.

- Make eye contact and listen.
- Be charming. Say "Hello" and "Goodbye" and all those other nice things your mom taught you.

Name Tag Placement

"My eyes are up here!" exclaims Tanya, fuming as she bolts to reconnect with her colleagues. "Can you believe this guy . . . he kept looking down my chest!"

Well, Tanya, your name tag is smack in the middle of your chest—uh, shocka-roo!

> For easy reading and fewer misperceptions, please place your name tag on your upper right shoulder. Keep your beautiful locks back. If you take your jacket off, reposition your name tag. Why? We introduce ourselves, but later in the conversation, when we forget who we're talking to, in a blink of an eye, we can glance down to refresh our memory.

Ladies: Please don't place your name tag on, right above, between, or just below your breasts (especially if you are wearing a low-cut top). Unless . . . well, that's another conversation.

This is an ideal example of why etiquette is so important. This simple practice avoids a number of embarrassing moments (having to ask someone to repeat their name, being accused of ogling, etc.). Simple, but quite effective.

The Lanyard/Clip Name Tag

The clip name tag: I'm not crazy about them. If you don't have the right collar to clip it onto, you're kind of stuck trying not to ruin a blouse or tie.

The lanyard name tag: On the plus side, you don't get sticky goo or clip marks on your clothes and they are easy to put on and remove. Unfortunately, I have to hunch down to tummy level to read it. That's not convenient if I forget your name. Also, it tends to get tangled as I reach out to shake your hand.

Some dilemmas just can't be solved.

Wandering Eye Guy

"I see I'm cramping your style."

When someone just isn't interested, pick up on it. Getting irritated or forcing someone to converse will make the networking experience unpleasant for you and for them.

Rosalinda Gets Personal:

I see a gentleman standing there, alone, with the complimentary glass of wine in one hand. In retrospect, his stance and roaming eyes clearly stated that his priority was not to make "business" connections.

I approached him, introduced myself, and put out my hand to shake his. He looked somewhat surprised, as he had to pass his wine glass from his right hand to his left. As I opened up the conversation, his eyes were not on me, but on every woman that walked by—he was on the prowl. After the third diversion, I had an "I just caught you looking" smile on my face ready for him. He had absolutely no interest in our conversation. I politely excused myself, and he bolted—probably towards his "target."

For some people, networking isn't about making business connections, it's about the free food and drinks, hooking up, or satisfying an obligation. It's kind of selfish and unprofessional, I'd say. Don't be that person. Utilize the opportunities that a networking event can open up for you.

From the Audience:

Q: I like to talk to as many people as possible at networking events. On a recent occasion, there was a gentleman who wouldn't stop talking. I attempted to end the conversation several times, but to no avail. How can I politely disengage from a conversation in the future?—Pam

A: Dear Pam,

The "sticky networker" can be a challenge. Obviously, you made them feel at ease. Here are a few options to consider for future sticky situations:

When he or she takes a breath, jump in with:

"Good luck. Please excuse me, I'm going to get something to drink." (Yes, they may follow you.)

"Why don't we go mingle with the others?" Walk up to someone or a group, introduce yourself and your "friend." Within a minute or two, excuse yourself from the group, leaving chatty-Chad to enlighten someone new. (A little sneaky, but effective.)

"Excuse me, please. I'm expecting a call." (Again, a little well-intentioned white lie.)

Extend your hand to shake, saying, "It was a pleasure to meet you. I don't want to keep you any longer; we are here to mingle. Please excuse me." (This is the most direct approach. It is important to not wait for a response . . . too late? Pull up a chair.)

Buy My Product . . . or Else!

It's business; sometimes you get turned down.

The if-you-don't-buy-I-won't-ever-talk-to-you-again syndrome is so junior high.

You've seen them, the vendor tables at networking events. I try to roam and visit the vendor tables, if only to learn about what's new in the world.

> When we get our way, naturally we show the world our best side. But when we don't, what do people see?

One woman in particular stands out in my mind. Her product was some type of healthy, pre-packaged beverage. During our conversation, she insisted repeatedly that I sample the product, even after I repeatedly refused. (Red flag?) Eventually, I gave in and reluctantly had the sip of her life-changing juice; we continued to chat. I took her card and thanked her.

Signaling me to come back, she asked why I didn't buy her product. I explained, as diplomatically as possible, that I

> A "no" today doesn't necessarily mean forever (well, it does if you're a pushy or pouty vendor). "No" just means that I now "know" about you and your product. I may not buy, but I may know someone who might. A potential client could overhear your tactics—if you are pushy, you might just lose another sale. I'll wonder if you will bite my head off if my order is too small. If I like your product, but not your style, you can be sure I'm looking out for another rep. Be nice, even if you don't get what you want.

would keep it in mind, but was not interested at this time. She insisted that I buy at least one; she reminded me that I had liked the flavor, that it was good for me, etc. She wouldn't stop.

Will I ever buy a product from her? Would you?

I understand that some people may be desperate for a sale, and I'm sorry for that.

At future events, the woman never spoke to me again. Now that's not nice, or professional.

> "Sales are contingent upon the attitude of the salesman—not the attitude of the prospect." —W. Clement Stone (American businessman, philanthropist, and author)

Six Possible Consequences of Playing the Pouty Business Person:

1   I will not do business with you. Ever.

2   I will not refer or recommend you to anyone. Ever.

3   We will not become friends.

4   I will not use services or buy products from anyone that you recommend. At the very least, I'll be extremely cautious and double check your referral.

5   I will politely decline to comment or say something very vague if anyone asks me about you or your products or services.

6   I will not be stopping by your vendor table again. Ever.

I wish you well and hope that you learn quickly that your sales technique could use a little modification.

> "If people like you, they'll listen to you, but if they trust you, they'll do business with you." —Zig Ziglar, American author, salesman, and motivational speaker

Five Simple Ways How *Not* to Annoy a Potential Customer:

1   Listen.

2   Smile.

3   Give them a brief pitch about the product they're interested in—not the one you want to sell—and stop.

4   If you can't deliver, don't promise.

5   If you don't have it, tell them who does. (Yes, even if it's your competitor.)

TRADE SHOW
DEPORTMENT

When you stand behind the banner, you are "on the clock," representing your company and yourself.

In most cases, a professional appearance and demeanor creates confidence in the consumer. Follow your company's protocol.

Look at this as an opportunity to show your boss that

you are the go-to person. You give your best under all circumstances.

If you are the owner, it's your image.

The purpose of spending oodles of dollars for a booth and all of the banners and giveaways is to increase sales! With that in mind, here are a few things to consider when you are the person behind the booth:

Behavior

- Behave yourself. What they see is what they assume—good or bad.
- Grooming, picking your teeth, adjusting or scratching your body parts, or re-tucking your shirt should be taken care of in the nearest restroom.
- Introduce yourself to the neighboring booths.
- Rubbernecking when a good-looking guy or girl strolls by will not make a good impression on a potential client. (A quick glance, maybe, but no drooling or cat calling, "Hey, hot thang!")

Cell Phone Use

Limit it. People might walk by because you are not available. Or maybe they will think you aren't someone who wants to bother with a prospective customer; they'll feel like they're intruding. (That's *not* what you were sent there to do!)

If you need to make or take a call, walk away from the booth. If you're a one-(wo)man show, wait for prime time to cease, or make it short and sweet.

Would your boss be happy seeing a photo of you in front of the banner chatting away or hunched over browsing through your phone?

Posture

It can be grueling on the feet to stand all day; it's better to take breaks away from the booth.

If you do sit, sit up straight (like you have energy and love being there).

If you stand, stand up straight. Leaning against something is understandable; however, look up and smile. (Slouchy posture looks tired, bored, unprofessional, lazy, and apathetic. If you aren't gung-ho about what you're selling, why should I be excited about buying it?)

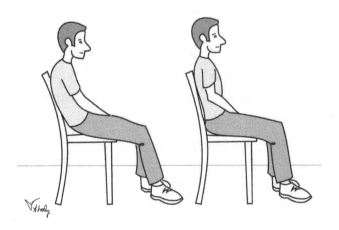

Which one would you want to talk to?

Voice Volume, Tone, and Topics of Conversation

Keep it professional and use your "considerate" voice.

Loud voices that can be heard two booths down may turn off passersby or a current client who may decide to "shop" elsewhere (and explain to your boss why).

Your tone and energy can make a difference to an interested passerby. (A blasé or hurried tone is a turn-off in business.)

Avoid discussing unprofessional topics with other exhibitors or booth buddies. This includes putting down competitors, complaining about being there, lack of business, or how drunk you got last night. (Sharing a few basic concerns, lack of attendance, and the like is normal; just don't get too depressing.)

Tardiness

There's no excuse (well, aside from an unexpected traffic detour, a flat tire, or an accident).

Arrive early, set up, and smile. (Your breakfast burrito should have been consumed prior to start time.)

An empty booth is a passed-over booth.

Patience

Have it. Yes, even with the long-winded person. Now, if you are neglecting other visitors, you may politely ask the person to return or say that you will contact him later to continue the conversation.

In the meantime, try not to let out a yawn or do the bobble-head nod—they will notice.

The "I-Only-Have-Eyes-for-You" Attitude

Don't assume, "They don't look like they'll buy." Even more consequential, don't let your attitude or facial expression say it.

Acknowledge every person as a potentially significant customer. (They might not buy this year, but they'll remember how you made them feel and come back or tell someone.)

Look at the person who's in front of you. Looking away or behind them says, "I'm checkin' to see if I'm missing anything." Make eye contact.

Avoid "yes" or "no" answers. Don't reply and look away. (Watch them walk away.)

Pigging Out

How can I talk to you when you've just shoved a massive bite in your mouth? I don't want to come close to that. I would feel like I was interrupting someone's dinner.

Walk away from the booth and enjoy your double-decker club sandwich or drippy salad.

How will you shake hands with passersby? They might walk past your booth for that reason alone.

Make a stop at the restroom to check between your teeth, pick through your mustache for crumbs, reapply your lipstick, and adjust your stuff.

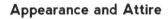
Appearance and Attire

The industry should be considered. But again, you can step it up a notch or two. Say it's a comic book trade show. I'm certain you'd see people "in costume" and expect a much more casual feel.

Clean clothes would be nice.

Shower. (You laugh! I know I've repeated this one, but it is more common than you would think.)

Maintain a presentable hairdo. (No matter what color or style, make your hair look combed and clean.)

Trade shows can be fun; it's in your attitude. You can make contacts (maybe even get a super job offer), learn more about your industry, get better acquainted with coworkers, and learn what your strengths and weakness are.

Think of it as a theatrical performance and you are the star! Be prepared, be confident, and look your best!

KEY POINTS:

- Always be aware of other people's schedules. Be on time and don't keep them past the agreed time (unless you both agree to extend it).

- Don't cause distractions during meetings—it's just annoying and it wastes everyone's time. No one will want to sit next to you at the next meeting.

- Let your personality shine through at networking events, conferences, and trade shows. Just keep it polite. You never know whom you might impress . . . or scare off.

- Eating or hooking-up should not be your priority when attending networking events.

- If your effort is minimal on how you present yourself, shall I conclude that you apply similar effort to your business, services, or products?

- Trade show booth guy/girl: What would your boss say if he/she saw you right now?

- Apologize when necessary.
- Learn to accept rejection with grace.

CHAPTER 6

WORKPLACE BEHAVIOR: IT STARTS WITH ME

....

WHAT I DO: THE POWER OF ACTIONS

If you love your job, you are fortunate. If you work in a place that fosters professional behavior, you are fortunate. If you work in a place that encourages a kind and friendly atmosphere, you are fortunate.

How much professionalism, kindness, and friendliness do you contribute? Because that is where it starts—with you. This chapter talks about the things you can do and say (or *not* do and *not* say) to maintain a courteous and respectful workplace.

17 Reasons Why Etiquette (and Common Courtesy) Matters in the Workplace:

> "The test of good manners is to be able to put up pleasantly with bad ones."—Wendell Willkie, corporate lawyer

1   It can improve a decaying atmosphere.

2   It can turn beastly attitudes into nice ones.

3   It builds trust with clients, coworkers, and management.

4   It will earn you respect.

5   It will gain you more influence.

6   It helps employees get along with each other.

7   It reduces hurt feelings.

8   It reduces misunderstandings.

9   It improves teamwork.

10   It diminishes the severity of unpleasant situations.

11   It improves listening skills.

12   It allows employees to handle dilemmas with dignity.

13   It will help you develop patience.

14   It sets a more respectful and professional tone.

15   It creates awareness of rude/childlike behavior and breaks bad habits.

16 It increases job satisfaction.

17 It makes work pleasant. (You won't dread Mondays anymore . . . or, at least, not as much.)

Bad Manners = Job Stress

Did you know that we take our work troubles home with us? No wonder our family doesn't drop what they're doing to rush to the door to greet us!

What is the solution?

Start with the basics:

Courtesy: Say "Please," "Thank you," "You're welcome" (However popular it may be, "No problem" is not the most appropriate response. Beating a dead horse?), "Pardon me," and the occasional, "I'm sorry." Magic words . . . do they ring a bell?

Consideration: Be aware of how your words and actions affect those around you. It's not all about you—at least, not in the workplace. Psst! It might be time to take down your "You're following a diva" bumper sticker or the "That's right, you're behind me" license plate frame. Just sayin'.

Respect: Listen to opposing opinions without interrupting. When someone's opinion differs from yours, refrain

---

Did you know that "job stress" often stems from rude behavior in the workplace and it costs US businesses more than 300 billion dollars annually? Christine Porath, assistant professor at the Marshall School of Business and co-author of *The Cost of Bad Behavior*, shows that contention in the workplace is related more to the behavior of coworkers than to the actual job duties. [7]

from name calling or mockery. By the way, this includes the unspoken rudeness: rolling your eyes, sarcastic chuckles, and exasperated sighs.

Tact: Know when to zip it. If you must remark, keep it factual and non-accusatory. Use discretion, and speak in a civil tone.

Humility: Don't confuse this with subservience or timidity. Accept criticism without becoming defensive. Don't engage in who-did-what conversations. Acknowledge others. Accept compliments. Apologize. And please drop the arrogant attitude.

Humor: No, I don't mean bringing in a whoopee cushion or brushing up on the latest "What did the rabbi say to the . . . " jokes. *Humor* here refers to your attitude and outlook. Are you resilient, cheerful, and not easily offended?

> How is your "civility" reputation? Remember: "Every man's work . . . is a portrait of himself, and the more he tries to conceal himself, the more clearly will his character appear in spite of him."—Samuel Butler, English author

These basic principles of etiquette are a simple recipe for a more productive, professional, and polite workplace. This is something you can take home to the family too.

As Jacqueline Whitmore says in her first book, *Business Class: Etiquette Essentials for Success at Work*, "Raw talent, education or experience, and competency are no longer enough to get a job, keep a job, and advance in a job."

How to Survive the "Cube Farm": Privacy Shmivacy

The term "Cube Farm" simply refers to a large space filled with a mass of partitions. Aside from its efficient use of space, the cubicle is supposed to provide the employee a little privacy, a nook to call their own, and a refuge from distractions. *Really? I can hear (and smell) your rustling chip bag.*

First of all, in the world of cubicle offices, people don't always expect or demonstrate the same courtesies as they would with a proper office with a door. Fortunately, there are steps you can take to establish similar boundaries. I don't guarantee they'll work, but you are welcome try them out.

Here are a few to consider:

- Request that the unexpected visitor knock, or gesture when there is no door. This not only awakens you from the trance that you're in from staring at your computer screen, but it also allows you a moment to discreetly minimize the screen (so they don't see you shopping for new patio furniture) or cover up any sensitive documents.

- Proclaim your boundaries. Calmly and in a matter-of-fact tone, say:

  - "I'd appreciate a 'knock' so that I'm not startled and unintentionally delete my work."
  - "Next time, please give me a call so that I can clear some time for you."
  - "Do you mind knocking next time? I like to imagine this is a 'real' office." (It could be awkward initially.)

- Do it with a smile. A sincere smile is important; it eases the tension and severity of the request.

- Use a sign, such as: "Please do not disturb." Do not overuse it; if you do, your coworkers may begin to ignore it. If someone does approach you anyway, stand your ground and say, "I'm sorry, but I'll have to get back to you this afternoon." If you don't enforce it, you might as well take it down. (There are exceptions; your boss, for example.)

- Introduce a new policy at the next staff meeting. Explain how these simple rules can create a more positive and less intrusive atmosphere. (Most of your coworkers will probably jump on board.)

Consider this: As with any change, give people a little time to get used to the idea, especially if you've always had a drop-in-anytime policy. Do unto others . . . sound familiar?

More cube-life tips:

- Don't walk away without minimizing your screen.
- Turn over sensitive documents.

- Call in advance.
- Knock. ("Do you have a moment?")

- If they look busy, walk away.
- Be aware of time.

- Maintain a professional tone.
- Do not discuss confidential matters. This includes weekend trysts.

- Don't toss your half-eaten curry wrap in their garbage receptacle.

- Don't be a snoop.
- Don't borrow without asking, and if you must borrow, return it ASAP.
- "I just have a quick question . . . " is still considered an intrusion when the "Do Not Disturb" sign is up.
- If you listen to ambient music, keep it down. (Not everyone enjoys listening to a babbling brook while they work.)
- Don't intrude on an existing guest.
- If someone is on the phone, don't plop down to wait; it might be private.

You may not have modesty issues, but don't assume that others don't.

- Don't make out or position your body in a flirtatious manner.

- Don't risk changing into or out of your gym clothes.

- Make every attempt to eat or snack away from your cubicle. (That's what the lunchroom is for.)

- Keep your cubicle decor professional. (A couple of family pictures are fine, but don't build a shrine to your children or an altar to Fido. Also, keep it G-rated.)

- Personal calls should remain personal—use an empty conference room or take it outside.

- Just because you can hear your "cube" neighbor doesn't mean you have license to comment on what they are saying or spread it around. ("Do not repeat anything you will not sign your name to."—Anonymous)

For the Pop-In Office Visitor or Anyone Who Doesn't Know When It's Time to Leave

Many people make friends in the workplace and may welcome a quick chat when their friends pass by their cube. However, when your friend is busy, he or she may not have time for an interruption. Use your eyes and ears! You are the intruder, remember? Watch for these clues so you know when it's time to clear out or keep on walking. You should leave and let them get back to work if:

- They don't stop clicking away on their computer.

- They pretend to be reviewing a pile of papers.
- They keep checking the time.
- They start to slouch in their chair.
- Their eyes glaze over (and not because they are captivated by your good looks).
- They are constantly adjusting their sitting position.
- They glance away . . . a lot.
- They have a blank look on their face.
- They call in anyone who happens to walk by.
- They are holding up their head with chin in hand.
- They are doing the bobble-head and replying with only "I see" and "uh-huh."
- They stand up. (Can they be any clearer?)

Most people don't mind being interrupted for a quick question—but keep it quick. This means no lengthy saga, follow-up questions, or "While I'm here . . . " topics. If anything, say, "I'm sorry for the interruption. Thanks for your time," and leave.

From the Audience:

Q: Ah, the perils of cubeland—when I worked in a cubical and wanted to focus on work, I'd wear my telephone headset all the time and simply look up at the unwanted intruder, put my fingers to my lips, nod, and listen intently to the nonexistent person on the phone with me. I'd also load my spare chair with work so no one could sit down—that always shortens visits. Both techniques worked most of the time. If not,

I'd smile and say, "Not now; I'm on a deadline."—Tanya

A: Dear Tanya,

Fabulous tips; and all within the boundaries of courtesy. Thank you.

Bummed-Out Bernard (B.O.B.)

"Any person who is always feeling sorry for himself, should be." —Anonymous

Do you see your coworkers scurry down the hall every time you turn the corner? Do your coworkers suddenly finish eating every time you enter the lunch room? Do your coworkers suddenly need to make an urgent call or hear their name being called every time you approach?

If you answered "yes" to any or all of the above, I'm sorry. Don't fret, though; there is something you can do about it!

To get to the bottom of the possible cause, ask yourself:

- Do I have a body odor problem?
- Does my garlic-pesto spread, anchovy-laced morning bagel have anything to do with it?

If you answered "no" to the above, then let's move on. Now ask yourself:

- Do I whine about the same old thing over and over again?
- Do I respond in a negative and woeful manner because there's never, ever anything good about "today"?
- Do I question a compliment, ask for proof, or

negate it with a "he's-better-than-me" comment?

- Do I complain about my job, pay, lack of love, the size of my television screen, or how I wish I could make myself go to the gym, over and over again?

- Do I perpetually spread scandal or share confidential news, only to compare it to my poor, pitiful life?

If you answered "yes" to any of the above, stop it! You may be Bummed-Out Bernard. Read the newspaper, watch a movie, read a book, take a class, take a walk around your neighborhood, or do something fun, interesting, or unique. This will give you something to talk about other than your semi-conjured-up, pitiful life.

In addition, it is super unprofessional to bring your woes into work. Naturally, from time to time, we all have troubles that carry into every aspect of our life—but not every day!

To the Coworkers of Bummed-Out Bernard

Although no one can make someone change—nor should they try, especially in the workplace—saying a kind word, listening to him once in a while, or ending the conversation with a "bright side" might help B.O.B. and help you in dealing with the bummed-out coworker.

We don't know why or how someone gets to a seemingly permanent state of self-pity. When you feel your patience running low, just think about how unhappy he must be. He is unable to find pleasure in anything that he does. Instead of rolling your eyes, give him a smile.

> ### Consider this:
>
> Bummed-Out Bernard: Unless you are under a binding contract, do you think you will be the one your boss thinks of first when it's promotion or salary (merit) increase time? Nope—it won't make you happy anyway; might as well give it to someone who will blossom and appreciate it. Your attitude affects your professional success or failure. Change your attitude today! Or maybe it's time to find a new job or join some kind of support group.

I'M ALL SHOOK UP

Office romance is not new. In fact, it's a convenient place to meet and develop a love interest. You spend five out of seven days with coworkers, and most of your waking hours. You see them at their best (you hope), and sometimes you get a glimpse of their personal side—perhaps at lunch or at the company party—all within the safe boundaries imposed by the HR department's policies.

While an office romance can be quite exhilarating, there are risks to this arrangement. What happens if the romance fades? Do you drag in the entire department to settle your lover's quarrels? Are you constantly using company time to send darling little love-texts? Do you take longer lunch breaks than permitted? What happens if you become their supervisor? Do you spend too much time in each other's workspaces? Are you sharing confidential information with each other? Are you declining projects that could help your career because it means working a little late for a few days? Are you neglecting your relationships with colleagues? Or, perish the thought, do you cover up for an indiscretion! You get the picture, don't you?

From the Audience:

Q: There's this guy at work, and he's really hot—totally my type. I haven't had a lot of luck meeting guys I like lately, and I really want to get to know him before some of the other femmes hook up with him. I've only told a couple of my co-workers that I'm into him, but I don't want everyone else to know—but still, I'd love to go out with him. How can I let him know? —Lulu

A: Dear Lulu,

Before I answer your question, I must first ask, does "hot" indicate a casual rendezvous? Or is there something deeper that you believe can turn into an everlasting love? If you are looking for a hook-up kind of relationship, work is the wrong place to look. There are too many possible repercussions.

Here are some options (if you insist on pursuing him):

- Invite him to lunch; see how that goes (he might not be into you; shocker, right?). Include a co-worker so there is less significance and tension.

- If it isn't too obvious, stop by his cubicle (knock and ask if it's a convenient time), introduce yourself, and talk about the company, where he worked before, etc. Keep it professional, and see where it goes.

- Finally, keep your eyes and ears open. He may flat out be telling you that he isn't interested. Take the hint, and don't embarrass yourself—talk about awkward.

Office romances require dignity, professionalism (don't do the dramatic head spin when you see him at the next meeting), and big-girl panties (no pun intended!). Don't get all "stalker" on him. Accept that he is not interested, and move on.

....

MULTI-GENERATIONAL COWORKERS

Today's workplace has several generations working together. This can and does create conflict. It can also be pleasant, enriching, dynamic, and even advantageous to you and the company. To me the strategy for getting along is simple—be respectful.

Eight Ways to Promote Cooperation:

1   Don't quickly dismiss an idea because the person who thought of it is too old/too young.

2   Don't treat her like you treat your mom just because she looks like she's about your mom's age.

3   Don't treat him like you treat your son just because he looks like he's about your son's age.

4   Learn from one another. Give in graciously if

their idea is better than yours.

5   Apologize if you initially made fun of their idea.

6   Don't make assumptions. Some young people have boring lives, while some older folks are out there experiencing new things.

7   **For the younger employee:** Adjust your attitude and your behavior. If a little more formality makes sense and is preferred, then do it. Conducting yourself in a more time-honored, traditional manner doesn't cost you anything or go against any principles, does it?

8   **For the older employee:** Adjust your attitude and your behavior. If a little less formality makes sense and is preferred, then try to do it. (Give 'em a break.) Occasionally overlook the quick cell phone check. Express your needs when they display a breezy attitude about deadlines.

....

WHAT I SAY: THE POWER OF WORDS

Everyone Likes a Compliment

> "I can live for two months on a good compliment." —Mark Twain, American author

Common reactions to receiving a compliment:

It's uncomfortable. I never got any growing up. I don't know what to say. I always feel like I have to give them a compliment back. I don't want to come across as arrogant. Etc., etc., etc.

Dismissing or diminishing a compliment is like turning away a present. Even when you don't like the present, you put on a smile and say "Thank you," right? It's the same with a compliment.

Giving the kind chap the brush-off can give the impression that you are unappreciative, ungracious, and unsociable.

Refrain from complimenting your coworkers' body parts.

Rosalinda Gets Personal:

After getting my hair done, I bumped into a colleague. After the routine greetings, she stated, "Oh, you got your hair done." And? Nope, that was it. My point? That was not a compliment, only an opportunity to show me her rude side or make some point. "If you can't say something nice . . ." I think you know how it goes.

Recommended replies when you receive a compliment:

- Thank you.
- Thank you very much (if the compliment was grand).
- Thank you. I appreciate it.
- How kind of you to say. Thank you. (This one's a bit formal, but nice.)

Try not to say phrases like, "This old thing?" "It was just a fluke," "I had nothing to do with it," etc. They only diminish the compliment-er's "gift" and tells him he has bad taste or doesn't know what he's talking about.

Ooh, You Said a Bad Word!

Cussing at work is, or used to be, considered highly unprofessional. Today, a slip of the tongue now and then is overlooked—but not when it's the only adjective you use. (Need a thesaurus?)

What message do you send when you cuss your head off? Here are a few possibilities: You are vulgar. You lack self-control. You have no consideration or concern for others. You lack judgment. You lack etiquette. You lack concern for your professional reputation. Your vocabulary is limited.

Cussing your head off might quickly appease your fury, but it is only temporary. Without calmly and logically discussing the issue at hand, the incident will surely escalate or repeat itself.

Think about it: Are you the one your boss will think of when it comes to wining and dining an out-of-town client? Will the boss trust you enough to put you in charge of a project? Or send you to a conference or training to represent the company?

And, if you're the manager, you might have a grievance slapped on you for offensive language.

Final tip: Just stop it! When the words slip out, apologize to your coworkers. Sign up for anger management or broaden your vocabulary. Instead of, "It was freakin' (you know what I really mean) awesome," insert *beyond, really, totally, far-out* (so 70s, but you can trend it), *hyper, super, exceedingly, ultra, sensationally, way, primo* . . . you get it, right?

La, la, la, la, la, la, la . . . I can't hear you.

Unclear and Uncertain Terms

Slang: 1. a language peculiar to a particular group; 2. an informal, non-standard vocabulary composed typically of arbitrarily changed words and extravagant, forced, or facetious figures of speech. [9]
    Let it go: Bro, dawg, dude, like, really?, you feel me, give 110%. (Okay, I'm horrible at math, but I don't think this is possible.) Think outside the box. (Isn't that just "thinking.") Literally, just sayin'. (I should remove this one; I love using it.)

It is not necessary to incorporate every trendy word that pops up into your business vocabulary. However, being aware of the new terms can help you engage better with younger coworkers.

Say What You Mean!

As a professional, you want to avoid or curtail these terms and phrases whenever possible. It can help minimize uncertainty and misunderstandings in the workplace.

Seriously? You know *I'm* Edward, right?

- "Whatever." (Really means: "It's not going my way" and/or "I don't' really care.")
- "It doesn't matter to me." (Really means: "I don't want to commit" and/or "I really don't care.")
- "I might be able to." (Okay, so when can I have your decision?)
- "Probably." (Oh goody! When will you be able to confirm?)
- "I don't know." (Uh, would you please find out?)
- "I'm not sure." (Can I provide you with additional data or information to help you be sure?)
- "That is a good question." (Would you tell me if it wasn't?)
- "Like . . . " (Just stop it!)
- "I can't deal with this right now." (When can you?)
- "Touch base" (Touch what?)

- "Let's take it to the next level." (Are we playing a video game now?)

Consider this:

When you reach a certain age (and I'm not giving you a number), you may want to adjust your vocabulary—especially at work. It's unprofessional and totally, like, embarrassing. You feel me?

I Heard It through the Grapevine

"A loose tongue will often get you into a tight corner."—Anonymous

---

You know when it's gossip: "You're not going to believe what I just heard?" "You've gotta swear you won't tell anyone." "Are you alone?" "If you repeat this, I'll deny I told you." "Guess what?"—all indicators that your coworker is about to spill some juicy gossip.

The custom of gossiping is here to stay. Some people thrive on it, while others are hurt by it.

Gossip may help you gain temporary popularity, but it's just not worth the long-term effect on your reputation.

What gossiping says about you:

- You can't be trusted with information.
- You'll talk about anyone.
- You don't consider the impact or consequences

of your actions.

- Facts are trivial to you.
- You probably aren't getting your work done.

What gossiping can do to the unsuspecting subject(s):

- They may be forced to prove a rumor untrue.
- Without their consent, a private matter was made public.
- They may receive confusing and inexplicable reactions from colleagues.

"What you don't see with your eyes, don't witness with your mouth."—Jewish Proverb

Be a gossip stopper. Most workplaces have an office gossip. Arm yourself with a gossip-stopper phrase or two. As they lean in to share the juicy hearsay, you can soberly reply:

- "I don't have patience or time for innuendos."
- "I'm not interested; gossip is never reliable."
- "She's a really nice person—I don't want to hear this about her."
- "Wow, I'd hate to hear what you say behind my back!"
- "I'm seeing him later. Do you mind if I tell him about this?"
- "My life is stressful enough. I don't need to add to it with all of this gossip."
- "Stop right there—I try to avoid all drama."
- "Let's go see her right now. That way we can get her version first-hand."

If none of the above phrases suit you, try walking away or changing the subject.

> "Trying to squash a rumor is like trying to unring a bell."—Shana Alexander, American journalist

INDUSTRY SPECIFIC

Outside Sales

- Give me your pitch; I expect it. But then allow me to ask questions.
- Don't dismiss my question just because you think you've answered it, you think it's dumb, you think I wouldn't understand the answer, or you think it's unnecessary for me to know.
- Don't bad-mouth your competition. Tell me why you are the best.
- Check in after you've made the sale (if applicable).
- It's okay to follow up, but don't hang up on me because I've decided not to buy. (Now I never will, and I'll have to tell my neighbor whom I just gave your card to.)
- Don't take a call when you are talking with me, especially if we've made an appointment.

Hair Stylists and Salon Professionals

- Don't check your texts while you're doing my

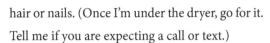
hair or nails. (Once I'm under the dryer, go for it. Tell me if you are expecting a call or text.)

- Don't look up to see who walked in the door as you are about to use the clippers. (That's my hair you are about to cut off!)
- Don't promise me something you can't deliver.
- Please keep your station and brushes clean.
- Please don't eat and cut, and please pop a mint after lunch.
- Disclose all the fees for your services *in advance*.
- Don't talk to someone across the salon; my ear is right there.
- This isn't time for "your therapy session." (Unless I ask you, I'm here to relax, not solve your problems.)

Doctors and Therapists

- Don't loudly state the purpose for my visit. (Remember a little thing called "privacy"?)
- Don't ask me to disclose my last bowel movement, cycle, or any other private bodily function in front of everyone.
- Don't roll your eyes while you're on the phone with a patient. (Is that what you do when I call?)
- Try to use a calm and caring tone; you are in the "caring for people" field.
- Don't figuratively pat me on the head and tell me it's all in my mind.

- I trust you. I believe you. Is that the same advice you'd give to your own mother?
- If you are running behind, please inform me when I check in. (I should have the option of waiting or rescheduling; everyone's time is valuable.)

Health Care Professionals

Patients look to you for encouragement, nurturing, assurance, and a compassionate and gentle demeanor—that's an order not everyone can deliver.

Nurses, EMTs, or anyone in the health care profession are to be admired. I believe it is a calling.

> "Let us be anxious to do well, not for selfish praise but to honor and advance the cause, the work we have taken up . . . to be more useful and helpful to our fellow creatures, the sick, who most want our help."
> —Florence Nightingale, founder of modern nursing

Please keep these things in mind:

- If you're exhausted, I'm sorry, but please take a break, take a day off, sleep, drink some coffee. From a patient's standpoint, you are more likely to become impatient and make a mistake.
- If you just can't stand what you do, I'm sorry, but please don't take it out on me, your patient. Until you can make a change or transfer out, you'll have to dig deep to find a professional attitude, or perhaps re-read the code of ethics.

- I can hear you. The canvas curtain is not soundproof.
- I may look asleep, but I might not be.
- Prudence: keep it professional; keep it confidential; keep it kind.
- I don't want to hear you speak unkindly about other patients, doctors, or nurses.
- I don't want to hear you complain about your hours, how bored you are, or how overloaded with patients you are.

Thank you, to nurses everywhere. I must give a special mention to my daughters-in-law, Kelly (Cory) Randall and Jonnalyn (Hernandez) Randall, who exemplify the best of the nursing profession: compassion, dedication, and conscientiousness.

Customer Service Staff

This includes receptionists, front office staff, restaurant host/hostess, and department store/boutique staff.

- I see you first—you set the tone for my experience. (That's a huge job and responsibility—please don't take it lightly.) You have the power to make my experience pleasant or unpleasant.
- If I annoy you, it's your job to make sure I don't know it. (I'm sorry about the customers who treat you like a peon—don't clump us all together.)
- You should always be happy to see me—without "me," the business fails, and you lose your job.

(Make me want to come back.)

- Smile and acknowledge me (a nod will do)—I will be happy to wait until you are able to help me.

- While you are assisting me, please don't complain to the cashier next to you about your break time, how you have to stay late, or that so-and-so didn't stock the socks correctly. (That is private company drama—customers don't like hearing it.)

- Don't make me wait until you finish checking your text (which, by the way, is probably against policy), finish your conversation with your coworker, or finish folding the stack of new inventory.

- If you hate your job or the company, look for another job! In the meantime, fulfill your duties—you did agree to them when you took the job!

> Dear bank teller: You placed saliva on your thumb to be able to count out my cash withdrawal. Please ask your branch manager to break down and buy a sponge and cut it up in one-inch pieces so that every teller gets one. Every morning, pour a little water on it and use it. Why? Because when you handed me the cash, I felt your saliva still on my bill. Gross.

....

"THE ART OF GETTING ALONG"

Sooner or later, a man, if he is wise, discovers that life is a mixture of good days and bad, victory and defeat, give and

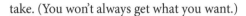

take. (You won't always get what you want.)

He learns that it doesn't pay to be a sensitive soul—that he should let some things go over his head like water off a duck's back. (So, what? They don't like you and they put you down? Move on; it's only an opinion.)

He learns that he who loses his temper usually loses (and looks the fool).

He learns that all men have burnt toast for breakfast now and then, and that he shouldn't take the other fellow's grouch too seriously. (It's not always personal; you just happened to be there.)

He learns that carrying a chip on his shoulder is the easiest way to get into a fight. (Let it go or learn how to accessorize your chip so no one has to see it.)

He learns that most people are human and that it doesn't do any harm to smile and say "good morning," even if it is raining. (Try living without the rain.)

He learns that most of the other fellows are as ambitious as he is, that they have brains that are as good or better, and that hard work, and not cleverness, is the secret to success. (Earn it.)

He learns that it doesn't matter so much who gets the credit, so long as the business shows a profit. (It's called being humble.)

He comes to realize that the business could run along perfectly without him. (Quit being so bossy; they get it already.)

He learns to sympathize with the youngsters coming into the business because he remembers how bewildered he was when he first started out. (Have patience.)

He learns not to worry when he does not make a hit every time because experience has shown that if he always gives his best, his average will break pretty well. (Don't spend time feeling sorry for yourself or blaming anyone.)

He learns that no man ever won a baseball game alone, and it is only through cooperative effort that we move on to better things. (Acknowledge those who help you.)

He learns that the fellows are not any harder to get along with in one place than another and that "getting along" depends about 98 percent on himself. (It's all in the attitude.)

—Anonymous

KEY POINTS:

- Treat everyone with significance and dignity, no matter how they behave.
- Tact and civility cost you nothing to use, but the cost is revealing if you don't use them.
- You aren't getting paid to "express yourself"; you're getting paid to do a job and do it well.
- Before you lose your temper, find a way to control it.
- You are in control of yourself and no one else. You can, however, be an influence. Set the tone for a professional and courteous workplace.

C H A P T E R   7

COWORKER QUIRKS AND DILEMMAS

....

COWORKER LOTTO

You don't get to pick your coworkers. If you're lucky, you click; and if you're not, you might be stuck working with the most impossible personalities. But, because you are a professional, you will find a way to get along.

"Why should I have to put in all the effort?" you ask. Well, it will make your life at work less stressful and poisonous, it's the professional thing to do, and most significantly, you have no control over their behavior, just yours.

Sometimes the solution is to adjust your ways, overlook minor infractions, and hope the coworker was just having a bad day.

Most people don't intentionally want to harass you or make your life miserable. In fact, I believe that most people want to be nice and liked by everyone.

There's one more thing to consider. The things you find discourteous, they may not; it seems to all be relative.

Politely, discreetly, tactfully, and respectfully approach all situations. By the way, you might find that it's not always "them"—we've all got our quirks.

....

GETTING TO KNOW YOU

Social Situations with Colleagues

From the Audience:

Q: I don't work directly with "Orlando," but we attend the same meetings, say "Hi" when we pass in the hall, and have had lunch in a group setting. He seemed to be a regular guy.

It just so happened that we were invited to a mutual colleague's birthday party; spouses or dates were also invited. My wife and I happened to sit at the same table with Orlando and his date.

During the party, Orlando seemed to be a different guy. He made snide remarks to my wife about other guests, hoarded the buffet line, and was generally disagreeable. He wants to get together socially—how do I discourage that?—Tim

A: Dear Tim,

It isn't that unusual for people to let their hair down when they're off the clock. It allows you to see the other aspects of their personality, which can be pleasing or disappointing. You did not mention whether alcohol was involved, which could have helped unveil the ornery side of Orlando.

Either way, you're in a jam. You could always try the avoidance method and hope with time he forgets about it. Here are a few other suggestions:

- "Sure, but we're pretty booked up for the next couple of months." (If you have children, that is probably the truth!)

- "Orlando, I try to keep my personal life separate from my work life; in my experience it works best that way." (This could get ugly if you go out with other coworkers and Orlando finds out.)

- "I think we'll just have to go to lunch once in a while; my wife has a lot going on right now."

- "We're keeping it low-key these next few months." (Just hope that Orlando doesn't see your fun-filled weekend posts on social media.)

- And then, there's the cold-hard truth: "Orlando, I just don't think we have too much in common, so let's just keep it between us here at work."

No matter which route you take, end it with a "thanks for the invitation," change the subject, get up as though you were walking away, and hope Orlando is a reasonable person.

Can I Give You a Lift?

It's raining, and your coworker is hopping on their bicycle (or walking) to make their way home. You offer them a ride; they decline. You insist, they resist. You finally take the hint and stop offering.

Sometimes people do things we don't understand and even find perplexing.

Did you ever consider that the cyclist is working on breaking a record, loves the rain, enjoys the solitude, needs to run errands, or can't tell you where they live?

Sober-living, safe house, halfway house—all must remain confidential. In many cases, even family members are not allowed to know the exact location.

P.S. Don't assume that everyone who declines a ride is living in a safe-house.

Carpooling Colleagues

Carpooling has its benefits: you can save money on gas and wear and tear on your car, you can catch up on reading, catch up on a sleep, reply to emails, and get better acquainted with coworkers.

The drawbacks can be getting better acquainted with coworkers, not liking the music selection, not being able to run errands during lunch, being stuck until the end of the day when the boss tells you to take off a little early, and not being able to get to your child if there's an emergency. And, unless you are the driver, you have to keep quiet about their driving style.

From the Audience:

"Kenneth" just joined our carpool. The problem is that his breath knocks us out every morning. We'd like to tell him, but some of us work with him, making it uncomfortable to broach the matter. We've tried cracking the window, but he's always cold, and asks us to close it. How can we handle this?
–Dolores

Dear Dolores,

This is a foul dilemma. "Morning breath" spares no one. It can be ever-so more malodorous depending on the previous night's menu. Here are a few options:

- Crack the window and switch on the heat. (Or, bring along an afghan to keep Kenneth cozy.)
- Bring a box of mints. Say something like, "Oops, I forgot to brush my teeth this morning . . . anyone else?" as you extend your arm towards Kenneth (hope he accepts).
- Offer Kenneth a granola bar or other treat to mask the m.b. (hope he accepts).
- Privately speak to Kenneth. Use the "it-hap-pened-to-me" strategy: "When I started carpooling, I realized that everyone suffered from my fifty-clove garlic chicken breath . . . someone told me, so now I'm really aware and just wanted to tell you" (hope he gets it).

Other tricky carpooling dilemmas:

- The chatterbox (and you like quiet): wear head

phones, sleep, read, or just kindly explain to everyone that you are not a "morning person."

- The unbathed: open a window, pin a fabric softener sheet to your shoulder (I've done this. Strange-looking but it really does help), speak to him/her privately and just be honest, look for a new carpool group.

- The pungent breakfast eater: crack the window, squirt a little room spray, ask them to eat it upon arrival.

From the Audience:

Q: There is one person in our carpool group that is always late. We have to honk at least two to three times before she comes running out with shoes in hand, makeup bag, and her coffee mug, which she hands off to me to hold for her while she puts on her makeup.

Last week, we were all late to work. We want to kick her out of the group. How should we tell her? –Luis

A: Dear Luis, It probably won't be a shock to her if you ask her to find another carpool group. Speak to her privately, but do it right away to give her time to find another mode of transportation. Ideally, a thirty-day notice would be nice; however, under the circumstances, a two-week notice should be enough. I say this because her tardiness is detrimental to your good standing with your boss. You might consider mentioning the situation to your boss since the potential of being late again is pretty high.

In the meantime, you can also implement a new policy.

Inform the tardy colleague that you will drive off without her if she isn't ready on time. No idle threats, Luis—be sure that you and the others are prepared to do it if you say it.

It all comes down to consideration for others and using tact when you approach a dilemma. And, honesty is usually the best policy.

The Uninvited Office Guest | Ginger Settles In

Here she comes again . . .

Oh no, here comes Ginger . . . I'll just look busy, maybe she'll keep walking . . . "Hi, Ginger." The "Please Do Not Disturb" sign goes unnoticed.

The signs are there; she never leaves. She unbuttons her jacket, pulls up her sagging left bra strap, and even whips out a half-eaten nutritional meal bar. What do you do?

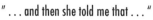
" . . . and then she told me that . . . "

Short of asking the uninvited guest to leave, you could take a kinder, more diplomatic approach. Here are a few suggestions:

- "As interesting as your recent root canal experience was, I have to get this letter out by noon."

- "I need to make a call; would you please excuse me." (Careful, she might not understand.)
- "Why don't I call you when I have time?" (Hopefully she doesn't insist on the time.)
- "Perhaps we could schedule lunch next week." (If she takes you up on the offer, bring along a couple of other coworkers.)
- "I was just leaving." Get up and walk out with her. (This is incommodious, but effective.)

If you entertain Ginger for even a moment after you've confidently and firmly stated your excuse, you might as well park it and settle in. Typically, the office yenta doesn't take a hint, and her keen senses tell her when there's a weakness or an opportunity.

What should you do when the office yenta settles in for a nice long chat? Well, you could hand him or her a "cold shoulder" sandwich.

Giving a guest the "cold shoulder" (of mutton) was customary in the early nineteenth century. Welcomed house guests were given warm meals at the beginning of their stay; however, if they overstayed their welcome, they were served a platter of cold mutton shoulder. After several meals of this, even the most stubborn guests would be ready to leave.

Aside from this visit taking up valuable time, you are encouraging the office yenta to continue the idle chit chat. Listening to office gossip is participating in office gossip. Of course, a few moments of inconsequential chatter is fine; it maintains a civil and cordial relationship with the office butterfly. You are in control of your time. Use it wisely.

If being frank with her or anyone like her isn't easy for you, I encourage you to try it. Most people are quite capable of handling a straightforward request, especially in the workplace. Just use a civil tone and say it with a smile.

Consider this: When you encounter a person who has no regard or clue, your only recourse is to use an authoritative voice to make your request; keep it short and simple. Stand when you say it—it has more impact. If you need to soften the request, you can certainly promise to stop by to visit them later.

TMI: I Don't Want to Know!

Do you enjoy sharing your life story? Write a book!

I'm sorry to inform you, but not everyone cares or is comfortable hearing about their coworker's personal "stuff."

I am not referring to your weekend activities, your child's new driver's license, or the new movie you saw. However, when you get into the details of your family dispute, how your girlfriend got plastered, the persistent oozing from the pimple on your hip, or your unpaid bills, it can become awkward for the listener.

If you do share this information, make sure the person wants to hear about it. Make sure they aren't going to include it in next month's office memorandum, and that it won't affect how they view you professionally.

Friendships form in the workplace, and they can be wonderful. Implementing and agreeing on boundaries while at work can help both of you professionally.

From the Audience:

Q: Our company lunchroom is average in size. Basically, you can hear most of what everyone is saying. One day, "Sigmundo," whom I consider a friend, was chatting away about a family issue—everyone was chiming in with opinions, so I did, too. Since then, he has avoided me other than a cordial nod. Do I say something?"—Rex

A: Dear Rex,

My guess is that Sigmundo did not like your opinion. Either that, or you solved his dilemma, taking away from his story. In most cases, when people openly share a dilemma, they aren't always looking for a solution; they may be venting or perhaps seeking affirmation of how "right" they are.

If you openly (publicly) talk about something, expect people to chime in. If you don't like it, find a private place.

Of course, you can have a face-to-face and point-blank ask Sigmundo what's up, or you could approach Sigmundo the same way you always have; if he doesn't respond, just be nice and move on.

Disliked by a Coworker

Reality: not everyone is going to like you. Do you like everyone you meet? Go ahead, dislike away, as long as you treat them in a civil manner.

A social acquaintance is easy to distance yourself from, but not so in the workplace. In fact, you might be paired with this unpleasant creature to work on a project or on the line right next to you. What are some options to help everyone get along?

1   Sit by them during break and strike up a conversation. You might find you have some things in common. (If they move away, don't follow—that's creepy.)

2   Formally ask to meet privately; include an unbiased third party. ("Let's see if we can talk things out.")

3   Decide to do your job, keep it civil, and ignore any animosity you feel from him or her. (This is difficult and draining, but doable.)

4   Greet them every day (the old kill 'em with kindness route).

The "He's Fabulous" Referral

A referral is a delicate and risky enterprise. You meet. You aren't impressed.

Imagine this: you casually mention to a few coworkers that you're in the market for a realtor. You see your coworker eagerly flipping through their ragged desktop Rolodex (Does anyone still have one?); they write down a name and phone number. They go on and on about how fabulous their experience was. In fact, after the business transaction, their relationship blossomed into a beautiful friendship . . . "You'll just love him," she says.

Naturally, you feel obligated to contact the referral, even though something in the pit of your stomach is saying, *No, don't do it!* Maybe you put off making contact, hoping that your coworker will forget all about it . . . no such luck.

You make the call. Immediately, you know this isn't the person for you, but you schedule an appointment anyway. You meet. It is confirmed—it isn't a match. How do you get out of it?

Options include:

- Schedule a phone interview with the realtor, instead of meeting in person (saves time). Don't commit. Thank them for their time and say that you will contact them if you decide to use their services.

- Tell your friend or colleague that you already have a long list of recommended realtors. To shut them down, conclude by saying, "If they don't work out, I know where to go."

- If your friend insists, tell them that you are looking for a specific style, location, expertise, etc.

- Tell your insistent friend that you have had too many unpleasant experiences with such referrals.

- Tell them that your spouse or mom just found the perfect realtor, and that it is settled. (If you approve of white lies, this would be the time to use one.)

Simply be honest from the beginning. Accept the referral; thank them and tell them that you will consider it. After all, they are only trying to be helpful, right? Hmm, or maybe earn a referral fee? Privately ask only those you trust for a referral. Research and interview potential experts yourself to avoid the situation in the first place.

Did I Ask You?

"You should use blah-blah instead of blah-blah?" Unwanted opinions seem to be a widespread bother. Most of us would like to respond with an emphatic, "Who asked you?" but we shouldn't. Most of the time, people are just trying to be helpful; take it as such and move on.

By the way, if we dig deep, we've probably offered our unsolicited opinion once or twice.

A simple "Thanks for the tip," or "I'll consider it next time," will suffice. They're happy, and you can maintain your sparkling reputation of being polite.

That's Personal!

From the Audience:

Q: What do you do when people ask personal questions? Sometimes too personal. How should I reply without sounding rude?—Carrie

A: Dear Carrie,

First off, you cannot control how people will react. Nor can you change it. Second, you do not have to answer personal questions.

Getting personal can happen with men, but generally speaking, it seems more prevalent among women. It's a way of finding common ground and becoming familiar. Most inquirers don't mean any harm; it's just their way of opening the doors of communication.

And in this "share-all" world, the thought of something being private or personal is becoming nonstandard.

I've reluctantly answered a question or two because I was too stunned to shut the nosy person down. Boy, I was peeved at them for asking. I should have been peeved at myself for responding!

Don't get caught off guard. Memorize one or two of the lines listed here (modify them to suit your personality).

Options:

- "That's kind of personal, don't you think?" (Most people will probably apologize right away.)
- "Do you mind telling me why you're asking?" (Ask only if you feel like being amused by hearing their reason.)
- "Do you really need to know?" (They may reply, "Yes, I do." Then you're stuck; proceed with the above phrase.)
- "I'm surprised you're asking; we barely know each other." (Snap!)
- "May we change the subject?" (or just shake your head and change the subject).
- "I'm sorry, I don't give out that sort of information."
- "Maybe I'll tell you when I get to know you better." (They won't know how to respond to that.)
- "Wow, people don't usually ask me questions like that."
- "What do you mean?" (This will make them explain; sit back and watch. Too evil?)

There is always that one person who won't take "No" for an answer and will try to strong-arm you into submission; repeat one of the above phrases and either walk away or lean in toward them, look them in the eye, and say, "That is too personal."

From the Audience:

Q: How am I supposed to get along with these younger employees who seem to be apathetic, whiny, and self-centered?—Willamena

A: Dear Willamena,

If you are referring particularly to "millennials," they have been labeled as you describe. However, you may come across this problem with coworkers of any age. You can't change people, no matter what generation, but here are three options to consider:

1   Set an example.
2   Create a guidebook on behavior policies.
3   Hire an etiquette consultant to present a workshop on tact and civility. (wink)

Maybe the lack of experience hasn't shown these young employees that certain traits and approaches used in their personal life are not applicable or welcomed in their professional life. They'll learn after a few hard knocks or the extended hand of a kind mentor.

P.S. Willimena, in case you haven't noticed, whining isn't reserved only for the younger generation. A whiner has no age boundaries.

> With every interaction and conversation, you are either building or destroying your reputation.

DISABILITIES

I'm Blind, Not Deaf

A person with a disability expects to be treated the same way you'd treat any other coworker. Obviously, be mindful of their restriction. Avoid making assumptions (and looking like a fool). For example, a visually impaired person is not automatically hard of hearing; please don't yell/talk at them. The preferred method to introduce yourself, shake hands, and hold a conversation with visually impaired people is to:

- Approach them, say hello, and introduce yourself.
- Give them a second to extend their hand for shaking. Take it and shake as usual. (They are blind, not necessarily weak and delicate.)
- If they don't extend their hand, you are welcome to say (or not), "I'd like to shake your hand."
- If they have an official attendant or companion, introduce yourself to them as well.
- Do not speak to visually impaired people through the attendant; that is rude and insulting.
- No matter what their disability is, don't freak out and apologize if you use common terms like,

"Does he come here often?"

"You should have seen the smile on his face," "You would have jumped too," or any other related phrases. They understand.

- Describe things. Describe how far to the door (not, "It's over there.")

- If you are going to walk away, tell them. If you are going to hand them a beverage, tell them. If someone else approaches, introduce them.

Wheelchair Sensibility

A person in a wheelchair, with rare exceptions, can hear and speak—just like you and me. Please don't make assumptions.

Here are a few key things to keep in mind when networking or working with a person who uses a wheelchair.

- It might be a temporary situation.
- Don't ask them how they got that way.
- Unless you are under ten years old, don't ask

them what it's like living "like that" or whether they wish they could walk.

- Don't ask them if they've ever tried getting help or suggest that they just make up their mind to walk.
- Don't share stories about how your brother-in-law took this herbal tea and the next day he was cured.
- Whenever possible, pull up a chair so that you can be face to face.
- Don't exclude them because they are "down there."
- Don't automatically get or do anything for them; offer first.
- Allow the same space you would with anyone else.
- Don't change the way you speak: "Would you like to go get a drink?" Please allow him or her to respond. (If you perceive a slight hesitation, you might add, "Since I'm headed that way, I'd be glad to pick one up for you . . . what's your pleasure?" You'd do that for anyone, wouldn't you?)
- Don't stand behind them in a group conversation. (They can certainly maneuver their chair to face you, but come on, it's easier for you.)
- Don't lean on their chair, hang your purse or jacket on the handles, ask them to hold your drink, or push them without their permission.

- Don't speak in a loud or exaggerated slow speech. (Embarrassing.)

People with visible and undetectable disabilities want to be treated the same as anyone else. If they need assistance, they'll ask.

....

COWORKER MILESTONES: AWKWARD AND OBLIGATED

Not Another Baby Shower!

Celebrations bring people together. They create a festive atmosphere, they offer delicious treats, blah, blah, blah . . . they drain your pocketbook!

Workplace showers, birthdays, and going-away parties: do you have to participate in every single one? The answer, of course, is no. However (you knew that was coming), if you want to develop or maintain an amicable relationship with your coworkers, you might consider attending as many as you have the time, money, and inclination to participate in.

Common sense dictates that if you didn't even know a coworker was pregnant, you can politely decline when the big manila envelope comes by. If you decide to give, don't feel obliged to toss in a twenty because everyone else did. If all you can afford is five dollars, then that's what you give—no need to provide a reason either.

By the way, if you didn't pitch in, don't even think about sneaking a piece of cake from the gathering. That will make you look cheap and underhanded, and you'll earn a reputation as a moocher.

From the Audience:

Q: My company adopted local families in need for Christmas. We were notified by email about this project. We were assigned teams. I was assigned to be a team leader.

I'm all for giving to the needy, but right now, I am practically in that category. First of all, I didn't have time to coordinate my coworkers, assign duties, and ensure it all got done on time. I ended up doing it, and of course, many of the coworkers on my team flaked out. To be sure the family got enough presents, I invested over 125 dollars, which was a hardship for me. What can I do next year or next time something like this comes up?—Daisy

A: Dear Daisy,

Just say, "No." Whether it comes from the boss, a colleague, or a client, a request beyond the scope of business is optional.

Next time, immediately meet with the project coordinator. Keep it simple.

- "I'm sorry, but unfortunately, I can't participate this year. "
- "Due to other commitments, I will not be able to help out. I'm sorry."
- "All I can do at this time is (fill in with a specific task you are able to do, and stick to it!)."

Don't feel obligated to share details about your financial status, time constraints, etc., unless you want to. If the coordinator insists, you do the same by repeating your statement, politely and calmly.

Bogus Bridesmaid

You hear that a coworker named Ariana is getting married. No big deal; you barely know her. The only thing that crosses your mind is, *Not another shower.*

Over the next couple of months, you seem to be bumping into Ariana more often—in the lunch room, in the parking lot, etc. One day, while you're tossing your purse onto the passenger seat, you hear her call your name.

Five minutes into the one-way conversation, you zone out. Then, all of a sudden, these words shake you out of your numb state: "Will you be my bridesmaid?"

"Oh, um, wow . . . " stumbles out of your mouth. She takes that as a "yes," and gives you the customary hug. Still stunned, you watch her walk away, still babbling about how much fun it's going to be and something about a list of duties.

If you're into cussing, this would be an appropriate time, but who would hear you? What do you do now?

> "A happy bridesmaid makes a happy bride."–Alfred, Lord Tennyson, English poet

Consider this: However you decide to handle this dilemma, do it tactfully and with a respectful attitude. Confab with a confidant, but keep it confidential. Don't spread the per-plexing encounter all over the workplace.

First, to avoid embarrassing her, speak with the bouncy bride-to-be privately. Also, don't devalue the invitation to be her bridesmaid. And almost as important, don't give her tons of excuses; that just opens the door to finding solutions to your excuses. Keep it short and sweet; oh, and honest too.

Best case scenario: She accepts without a coaxing battle.

"Thank you for asking me to be a part of your wedding party. I'm honored, but I can't accept." If she doesn't interrupt, you can continue, "I know that it will turn out beautifully." Whew!

Worst case scenario: "Oh, but why?" exclaims the bride-to-be, "You just have to. I need two more bridesmaids to make eleven, my lucky number! Why can't you?"

If you believe in telling "white lies," the excuses are endless.

You: Financially, I am not in a position to add another expense.

Bride-to-be: Oh, but the wedding is eleven months from now; you can save up!

You: I understand, but still, I am not in a position to add another expense. (Repeat, repeat, repeat. She will eventually get it.)

You: I can't commit that far in advance. I have a lot going on right now, and I'm not sure what my situation will be like by then. (It's ambiguous blather; hopefully it will be confus-ing enough to shut her down.)

Bride-to-be: Oh, well, do you know of anyone else around here that might want to be a bridesmaid? (And we're done.)

I'm Getting Married!

From the Audience:

Q: I've been working at my job for almost four years, so I've gotten to know a lot of my coworkers. Because our company is big, I don't often see a lot of them. Now that the word has spread that I'm getting married, these seldom-seen coworkers are always stopping by and asking me about my wedding plans. It's getting pretty awkward, especially since I don't plan on inviting them. One person even asked me for the date so she could mark it on her calendar. I'm not inviting her—or at least, I wasn't going to. I don't know what to do, and our wedding is nine months away!—Fabiana

A: Dear Fabiana,

Aww, even though it is a tad presumptuous on their part, how very heartwarming that your coworkers feel so close to you. Also, not everyone who asks about your wedding plans expects to be invited—now you are being presumptuous. Okay, that's probably not what you want to hear.

You could use your parents as an excuse. "Since my parents are paying for the wedding (or contributing generously), I have to stay within budget, and naturally that affects the guest list."

I am not a fan of feeling obligated to give a reason or an explanation to others. But sometimes it is unavoidable. "I'm sorry, but we have personal reasons for limiting the guest list," is simple, vague, and discourages further prying.

If it is untrue or you just don't want to drag your parents into it, here are a few more options:

- "We haven't thought about the guest list yet."
- "We'd be glad to include everyone, but you know how it is."
- "It's always difficult to exclude people we know."
- "It is going to be a struggle, with so many relatives on (his/her) side . . . "
- "We are having a small/intimate wedding."
- "Our budget doesn't allow for an extended guest list."
- "Thanks for your interest, but I don't want to spend too much time talking about my wedding . . . work to do." (I recommend this one. You are there to work.)

Use "we" as much as possible; this will remind the "non-invited" guests that you don't have the last say—it is a mutual decision between you and your spouse-to-be.

From the Audience:

Q: I received a business gift. Is it necessary to send a thank-you note?—Takumi

A: Dear Takumi,

Yes and no. If the gift is a gag-gift, promotional item, something small, or if you opened the gift in front of the gift giver, you do not need to send a note. Thanking them in person is usually enough. If the gift was purchased especially for you corresponding to a particular interest or activity, they went to great lengths to obtain it, or the gift was expensive, a thank-you note is advisable. Basic rule of thumb: if someone made the effort to think of you, spend money, or give of their time, writing a short note is a small way to express your gratitude.

Q: Is it acceptable to send a note of thanks via email? —Alicia

A: Dear Alicia,

There is something special and unique about a hand-written note. The answer is yes. My "yes" comes with strings attached. If you are thanking someone for lending a hand, taking you out to a casual lunch, a brainstorming session, or referring you to their barber, a brief note of thanks via email is acceptable. Texting is a last resort.

Q: Last year, a coworker gave me a gift, and I had nothing for her. It was awkward, and I didn't know what to do. I don't want to start a gift-giving relationship, but in anticipation, should I be prepared to give her something this year? —Ignacio

A: Dear Ignacio,

Most people give without expecting anything in return except for a sincere and cheerful "thank you." Perhaps she was grateful to you for helping her out with a project and this was her way of expressing her gratitude.

Regardless of her intention, you are not obligated to "pay her back." When you receive an unexpected gift, do not insult the thoughtful person with an endless diatribe ("Your gift hasn't arrived yet," "I left it in the cab," or "I think my room-mate ate it."). Accept the gift graciously, thank them for their thoughtfulness, and wish them a fabulous holiday. Consider sending a thank-you note.

P.S. I recommend you check the company policy on gift giving.

The Proud Parent

We've all experienced it, the proud papa sharing every last detail of Junior's first goal attempt. Or how their little Anna-belle is the most talented piano player that ever lived.

It's endearing, really.

Sometimes parental pride can blind your senses. Be aware of the signals that tell you it's time to stop.

From the Audience:

Q: Most of us in our department have children, varying in ages, so naturally we exchange news about our kids. How-ever, "Dwayne," who just started with our company, is one of those parents who only talks about how great his kid is.

The problem is that he interrupts our stories to tell us about how much better his kid did it or will be able to do it. We don't know how to make him stop. How should we handle the situation? —Leslie

A: Dear Leslie,

Sharing a bit of news about your child now and then is expected and quite common among coworkers. However, over-sharing (about anything) will eventually lead to aversion.

Options:

- When Dwayne takes a breath, quickly chime in with, "That's great, Dwayne, but let's let Martin finish what he was saying."

- Interrupt Dwayne. "Excuse me, Dwayne, but I don't think Martin was finished." (Of course, Martin could say it himself, but it is less forceful if someone else says it. This strategy probably won't work the first time. Implement every time he interrupts; he'll get it eventually.)

- Have a private confab. "Gosh, I see that you're really proud of Annabelle, as we all are of our children. We can get so caught up in their activities that we want to share every little detail. With such limited break times, we all try to share only the highlights . . . can you imagine if we shared everything (sincere chuckle)? We wouldn't get any work done. (This may or may not sink in. You'll find out soon enough.)

- Change the subject. I'm not suggesting that you rudely interrupt Dwayne and start talking about a random topic (tempting, but not nice). At an appropriate pause, simply introduce a new topic. "That's wonderful, Dwayne. So, did anyone watch the game last night?" "I'm thinking about taking a tai chi class; anyone interested?" Nothing about children.

It all comes down to this: You can pick your friends and your significant other, but you can't pick your coworkers. So what do you do when your cubicle mate is the creature from you-know-where? You deal with it using respect, tact, courtesy, consideration, humility, and a splash of humor. And secretly hope and pray that he or she gets transferred or decides to find a new job.

Ultimately, it is your professional reputation at stake. In the end, that's all you have left.

No one will remember the great report you turned in, or how you always refilled the copy paper bin, but they will remember how you made them feel.

So when you think you just can't take it anymore, get a breath of fresh air, visit a confidant, and focus on your reputation and integrity.

KEY POINTS:

- Don't be afraid to tell coworkers if they get too personal.
- Don't be afraid to say "no."
- Don't divulge details of your personal life; it could bite you in the derriere.
- Respect coworkers' time and space. Set a good example for them to follow.

CHAPTER 8

DINING BASICS AND WORKPLACE CUISINE

This chapter doesn't focus on fancy schmancy dining etiquette. However, I do recommend acquainting yourself with the formalities, which is why I've listed the basics.

Some people believe that table manners (or a lack of them) reveal a lot about a person. That is why many companies conduct the interview over lunch or dinner. This is especially true if the position you are being considered for includes dining out with clients. Your table manners divulge whether you will represent the company well. So, when the interviewer takes you out to lunch, what does he or she watch for?

Moderation: Do you take advantage when someone is picking up the tab by ordering expensive items, wine, desserts? Do you prefer to dine only at exclusive restaurants, etc.?

Composure: How do you react when something spills, your order is wrong, or the service is slow?

Attentiveness: Do you consider your dining companion? Do you pace yourself? Do you avoid monopolizing the conversation? Do you keep track of the time? Does your style of eating gross people out?

Posture: Are you slouching, reclining your chair, leaning back and undoing your belt buckle, or hovering over your plate?

A meal serves to nourish our bodies, but more than that, it provides a time to connect and socially engage, which adds to the pleasure of the meal. Too corny?

....

SMACKING SENDS YOU PACKING

Whether dining at a fast-food joint or a five-star establishment, there are standard rules that apply. For example, chewing with your mouth closed, not shoveling food into your mouth, not licking your fingers, and staying off your phone are all widely accepted rules of dining etiquette, no matter the venue. Eating with someone who exhibits any of these unappealing traits can quickly make you lose your appetite. Now imagine dining with a potential employer, your future in-laws, or a date; your first meeting may be your last.

Dining Quiz: How do your dining skills rate?

1   I am out with a group of five, but only one other person and I have been served. What do I do?

   A I take the opportunity to post a photo of my cobb salad.

   B I ask for a drink to take the edge off.

   C I wait until everyone is served.

2   I've been asked a question, but I just shoved a huge bite into my mouth. What do I do?

   A I hold up my forefinger indicating to everyone to wait a second.

   B I finish chewing, swallow, and then talk.

   C I place my napkin over my mouth and proceed to talk.

3   I dropped my napkin on the floor. What do I do?

   A I discreetly pick it up, hoping that no one notices.

   B I leave it there and hope I won't need to use it.

   C I leave it and ask the server for a new one.

Answers:

1   c. In a small group, you wait until everyone is served before you begin eating. The exception is if someone's order takes longer to prepare, then they should give the go ahead for you to start without them.

2   b. Take small bites, especially when dining with others. That way you can discreetly shift the bite to one side of your mouth so that you can briefly reply without making your dining companions wait.

3   c. Never pick up anything off the floor. (Germs! You can't put it back on the table.) Ask your server for a replacement. Naturally, if it's in the aisle, kick it under your chair.

Great that he's using the napkin, however, you don't lift the entire napkin off of your lap, just the top layer.

Top four reasons a dining interview fails:
1. Being rude to the server.
2. Arriving late.
3. Having poor table manners.
4. Being underdressed.

The Brazen Executives

What do you do when lunch becomes "a boys' night out"?

Q: I am a newcomer to the corporate world. I understand the importance of business lunches, which require extra work and attention to proper etiquette.

Recently, at a lunch with two company executives, I was appalled to witness the transformation from professional to a completely carefree attitude upon leaving the office. Suddenly, profanity and the discussion of sensitive topics (children, spouse bashing, sex) became commonplace.

During lunch with the executives, I remained quiet and observant, unfortunately giving off an uninterested vibe, which was not my intention. Could my lack of involvement been seen as a negative factor? Should I have acted differently?—Arturo

A: Dear Arturo,

My short and sweet response is, don't compromise your principles. This can be difficult to do when it is your superior.

There are a few options to consider:

- Accept their invitation on a less-regular basis.
- Offer alternate lunch choices. Eat and walk. (You can use the scenery to change topic of conversation.)
- Invite another coworker who can balance the conversation. In fact, invite a female coworker—that would rule out any risqué topics. (Naturally, you must clear the invitation with the executives first.)

- Have a few topics up your sleeve to change the subject. (They may or may not go for it.)
- Jokingly say, "Is that all you guys talk about?" or, "My friend's company sends you to 'sensitivity training' if they catch you talking about . . . "

Since you don't partake in the conversation, be prepared to be questioned or teased. "What's wrong with you?" "Dude, what's your story?" "Have you ever . . . ?"

This is the moment of truth. Join in or decline? Here are a few responses to consider:

- "I'm old-school; I don't kiss and tell."
- "Compared to you guys, my life's pretty dull." (This should work.)
- "If I told you, I'd have to kill you." ([insert nonchalant laughter])
- "I'm not seeing anyone right now." (Use this one only if it's true.)
- "She'd kill me if I talked about her." (This one is innocently misleading; it gives the impression that you would join their talk . . . if you were assured she wouldn't find out. It may have the opposite effect, though, and produce extra coaxing from the execs. Use with caution.)
- "Would you mind if we kept the conversation PG?" (Direct, honest, and risky.)

A business dinner or lunch should be treated as an extension of your job.

Lunch with the Boss

From the Audience:

Q: During a business conference, my boss offered to take me to lunch. I looked at it as an opportunity to get to know each other better. Tired of "conference food," he suggested we go offsite. Driving only two or three minutes from the hotel, we pulled into the parking lot—a male-focused dining establishment, where the uniform for mostly-female waitress staff is alluring.

I enjoy this restaurant as much as the next guy, but not as an expensed business lunch, and not with my boss.

I felt uncomfortable during the meal due to the scenery, which I was attempting to enjoy, but not to the extent that I would seem perverted. I was dancing a fine line between being respectful to my boss, discussing business issues, and glancing at the waitresses as they wandered by. The waitresses won.

I question the appropriateness of this business lunch. Should I have said something? As a man, if I would have said something, would my boss look at me as if I had lost my manhood?—Lamar

A: Dear Lamar,

It's not your expense report to worry about or explain. You learned more about your boss, didn't you? The choices we make in our business life can make or break our reputation. I am not saying that eating at a male-friendly establishment will destroy your chances of a promotion, but during business hours, choosing a more neutral place to dine is advisable (especially if female coworkers are present). As for your "manhood," it sounds like it is quite stable.

> If you love to post photos of your meal, go for it, however, not during a business meal.

Consider this when dining with the boss: Why has your boss invited you?

- In Lamar's case it was about the food and the ambiance. Use the time alone with your boss wisely. (Stay away from personal downer matters and sordid details.)

- Don't gossip about coworkers or whine about policies, job duties, the sub-standard cafeteria salad bar, or your paycheck. (That's a great way to never get invited out again.)

- Allow your boss to introduce topics of conversation. (Listen for clues and openings; it's okay to talk about your hobby, vacation, book, or classes—especially if you know your boss enjoys the same thing.)

- If he/she invited you, allow them to pick up the tab. (Don't make a fuss or pull out your gift card.) A simple "Thank you, Ms. So-and-so," is all you need to say. If it was their favorite restaurant, comment on it, the good service, the view, something.

- Keep your cell phone off and hidden. I'll probably

repeat this one. (Yes, even if the boss checks his/hers.)

Drinking on the Job

Obviously, I am not referring to pulling out a flask from your drawer and pouring a swig of coffee liquor into your latte! (If that's what came to mind, you might have a little, teeny-tiny problem.)

Lunches, dinners, time out with a client, or a company party are all opportunities to build your reputation, not to sensationalize or, worse, destroy it.

Remember that alcohol tends to loosen your tongue. (A business lunch is probably not the best circumstance to let your boss know what's what.)

From the Audience:

Q: I have a couple of drinks before company parties to take the edge off. What's wrong with that?—Ronald

> Hold your beverage in your left hand, leaving the right hand dry and available to shake hands.

A: Dear Ronald,

Oh, so they'll all be getting a different version of you? Look, tons of people "take the edge off," and that might be fine for social occasions, but in the business world, you need to be totally present. So what, you're a little nervous? You aren't the only one. Consider phasing out the use of alcohol as a means to overcome lack of confidence. Besides, what'll happen if one day there is no "edge-remover" available?

Consuming adult beverages is not a crime (unless you're under age)! Limiting yourself is just a wise career move.

....

DINING ETIQUETTE FORMALITIES (IN CASE YOU'RE INTERESTED)

Knowing which fork to use, how to properly butter your bread, or what to do with a finger bowl can't hurt.

My philosophy when it comes to the fine dining details is simple: if you are considerate (allow others to speak and watch your tone and volume), pleasant (show interest in others and avoid drama), and moderate (don't overindulge and don't disgust anyone), your dining companions will either overlook or not even notice if you pick up the wrong fork.

Business dining is about the relationship-building first, the meal second.

> "Sharing food with another human being is an intimate act that should not be indulged in lightly."—M. F. K. Fisher, American food writer

Why should you care about fine dining points? You might be invited to the White House for dinner. You might be invited to a corporate event. You might win the lotto, leading to a lifestyle of the rich and famous. Or, you might just want to be prepared to accept an opportunity with confidence.

The Napkin

Wait for the host to take his/her napkin before touching yours. (If he/she doesn't pick it up after a minute or two, take yours and place it on your lap.)

Do not unfold the napkin entirely. Keep it folded in half whether it's triangle or rectangle shaped.

Excusing Yourself: I had a third grader say to me, "It was gross when my mom's friend said she had to go pee."

Thank you, nine year old who knows that no one needs to receive an advance play-by-play when you excuse yourself to the bathroom—especially when you're at the dinner table.

"Excuse me, please," in a low voice is enough. If you're sitting with coworkers, a courtesy statement like, "I'll be right back," is more than enough. We get it. And if we don't, you'll be right back, so what does it matter.

Unfold the napkin below the table. (You don't want to knock anything over.)

The napkin will stay on your lap if you sit properly: legs together, feet flat in front of you. (It's called good posture.)

When you excuse yourself during the meal, where should you place your napkin? (In the etiquette world, there are a flurry of opinions on this one.) Options:

- Loosely fold it in half and place it on the seat of your chair or on the arm rest.

- If that grosses you out, place the folded napkin on the table, next to your dinner plate. This is not the best choice, in my opinion. However, if you choose to do this, I must emphasize folding the napkin soiled side in so that others do not have to see the wiped-off gravy.

- Sometimes, you don't get to decide. Don't be perplexed if upon your return your napkin is neatly refolded. Your server did it. (Just hope that his/her hands hadn't just been scratching something before they refolded it.)

Use the napkin even if you don't think you need it. Dab your lips before taking a sip of your beverage. (Backwash dribbling down the glass is very unappealing.) Unless it's a "lobster bib," do not tuck the napkin into your collar.

Did you know:

In ancient Rome, people often used two napkins each: one was tied around the neck and the other was used for wiping fingers. Guests brought one with them. At the end of the meal, their slave would use it to wrap up extra food. (Doggie-bag?) [11]

Dining Styles of Eating

There are two styles of eating: American (used by Americans only) and Continental (used by the rest of the world). Whichever you are more comfortable with, master it. Quite honestly, Continental style is much easier and smoother.

American style: After cutting a bite-size piece, rest the

knife on the upper part of the dinner plate. Switch the fork to your right hand (tines facing up) to pick up the newly cut morsel. Switch the fork back to your left hand (tines facing down), pick up the knife with your right hand, and repeat.

Continental style: After cutting the bite-size piece, rest your right wrist on the edge of the table (with knife in hand). Bring the fork to your mouth with your left hand, slightly twisting your wrist (tines facing down). Take the bite. While chewing, rest your left wrist (with fork in hand). Repeat.

Got Gristle?

You're enjoying a pork chop when you realize the piece you've been masticating for what seems like forever just isn't being crushed and mushed. What do you do? Expel or swallow?

There are two "etiquette–approved" methods:

1   Take your fork up to your mouth, as you would normally do. (This actually only works if you are eating American style.) With your tongue, push the unwanted morsel onto the fork. (Try doing this without going cross-eyed. Can you tell I don't like this method?) Bring the fork down to your plate and deposit the piece under a lettuce leaf or something. To avoid the tongue calisthenics, just swallow it.

2   Using your left index finger and thumb, quickly remove the morsel and place it under a lettuce leaf. Wipe your fingers on your napkin. (This is the preferred method.)

Do not attempt either method if you are engrossed in a conversation. No one wants to see this. If you find these methods awkward, you can excuse yourself to handle it in the restroom.

No, you cannot bring your napkin up to your face and deposit the chewed-up morsel. What will you do with it then? Dump it on the floor?

The Hanging Crumb

From the Audience:

Q: During lunch last week, my boss had a crumb or something hanging on his mustache. I wanted to tell him, but we were in the middle of a serious conversation, and I didn't want to interrupt him. I was glad when it eventually fell off; I could finally concentrate on what he was saying instead of watching and waiting for it to drop. What should I do if it happens again?—Burton

A: Dear Burton,

Forgive me while I chuckle. It is comical that we can become so captivated by something so minuscule.

In a group setting, telling someone about the hanging crumb is easier. There are more distractions; therefore, your signal will go unnoticed.

In a face-to-face situation, the untidy diner may notice the lack of eye contact and wonder. If the crumb in question looks like it will drop or the untidy diner uses his napkin frequently, you might wait. If not, then, at an appropriate moment, either discreetly gesture with your finger pointing to the "mustache area" and/or lean in and whisper, "You have something . . . "

Think about how you'd like someone to handle it if you were the one with the dangling crumb.

Blaine needs a refresher course:
Left arm resting on the table.
Right elbow resting on the table.
Needs to master the twirl.

FOODS TO AVOID AT BUSINESS MEALS:

Using good table manners allows everyone to enjoy the meal.

You and a few of your coworkers are meeting for lunch. It happens to be the rib shack around the corner. Enjoy.

However, if you're invited to dine at a plush, fine-dining establishment, you might want to avoid slurping and licking and wiping. Whether it's a business meeting or interview, selecting easy-to-eat foods will let you focus on the conversation, not the drip on your chin.

With so many menu options, I'm certain that you'll be able to select a more classic dish to enjoy, instead of:

Ribs. First of all, the chances are slim that you will find this item on the menu at a fine dining establishment.

"Why should I avoid them?" It's considered a finger food that requires using several napkins and sticky fingers, tearing meat off a bone, and wiping saucy cheeks—not the most genteel look.

Long Pasta. This menu choice is okay if you consider yourself a pasta-twirling pro. By the way, there seems to be a consensus: no *cucchaiaio* (spoon)! If you eat pasta, learn to eat it the right way—the Italian way. With your fork, take only two to three strands. While holding the tines against the side of the plate, twirl. It will take *practica*.

"Why should I avoid it?" If you don't twirl the noodles correctly, you will have to shove the huge mound into your mouth and feel the inevitable drip on your shirt, mustache, or chin.

Things with a Bone. Not recommended. It takes finesse to cut away from the bone.

"Why should I avoid them?" If you aren't careful when cutting, the boney goodness can slip off your plate. Unless you're at a rib shack, do not pick up the bone to suck the meat off. Sorry.

Double-Decker Anything. Avoid burgers, pulled-pork sandwiches, or the like. Again, it will probably not be on the menu.

"Why should I avoid it?" They are too messy, you have to open wide and shove it in, and your hands will be all sticky and drippy as you reach for your glass of iced tea.

How to eat a dinner roll: Place the pat o' butter on your bread plate. Break the roll in half. Break off a bite-sized piece from one half, butter it, and enjoy. Repeat. Unless it is a family-style restaurant, you eat only one bite at a time from your dinner roll. (Not worth the effort? Well then, you just saved a few calories.)

The Finger Bowl

The finger bowl is the upscale version of a wet wipe, akin to the hot towels provided in first class or sometimes at a Japanese restaurant.

Rosalinda Gets Personal:

On one of my first dates, I was taken to a posh restaurant. I knew how to behave at the table, but not how to use the seventeen (an exaggeration) utensils or the finger bowl. My date realized that I was bewildered by this pretty crystal bowl. One hand at a time, he slowly proceeded to dip his fingers, gently using his thumb to rub the others. While he brought one hand down to the napkin on his lap to dry the fingers, he proceeded to do the same with the other hand, making sure I did not feel embarrassed. What a gentleman.

Tableside Tips

Elbows: Don't. However, if it is a casual atmosphere and you are discussing business, you may place one elbow on the table and only between courses. Once the dish is in front of you, elbows off!

No more than your wrist should ever been on the table. (Uncomfortable, yet?)

Hats: Remove them, especially in a business setting. When and why did it become okay for a gentleman to keep his hat on? No, it doesn't harm or offend anyone, but removing hats at the dinner table was a nice tradition, a gesture that made the man and the moment special. One more thing: don't place it on the table; it may be sweaty, and there probably isn't room for it.

If there is an available chair next to you, place it there. If there is a hat rack available, place it there. If you travelled by automobile, leave it in your car.

Lipstick: Ladies, you want to come across as an equal and a professional, don't you? Don't apply lipstick at the table. Excuse yourself to the ladies room to apply.

Are there exceptions? Always. If you are with a familiar colleague, seated in the corner, and you two are the only ones in the restaurant, I guess it would be okay.

Toothpicks: Please don't pick your teeth at the table, nor on the way to the parking lot.

Pinky in the air: Please don't stick your pinky in the air. It all started way back before utensils existed. Commoners used five fingers to eat. In order for the nobility to distinguish themselves from the peasants, they used only three, leaving the ring and pinky fingers erect. We no longer need to do that. Today, it is considered pretentious.

The Toast

- If you make it, keep it brief and not about you.
- If the toast is to you, do not touch your beverage. (It would be like applauding yourself.)

- Return the toast immediately or before dessert is served.

- You do not have to toast with an alcoholic beverage; water, chocolate milk, or whatever you are drinking is acceptable.

> Clinking glasses when toasting is not really necessary. Originally the custom was to pour a bit of the guest's wine into your own glass and vice versa, to insure that neither had been poisoned. [12]

FORMAL PLACE SETTING

You know the number of courses by the number of utensils: With two exceptions (cocktail fork and butter knife), forks go on the left, knives on the right. You won't always encounter a formal place setting, but why not be familiar with it?

To easily remember which side your bread plate is on, use one of these two methods:

1 Make the "okay" sign using your thumb and forefinger, making a lower case b with your left, and a lower case d with your right. b = bread (left hand); d = drinks (right hand). (Preferably you can do this in your head—holding up your hands might look funny.)

2 Another way to think of it is, from left to right, BMW: bread—meal—water.

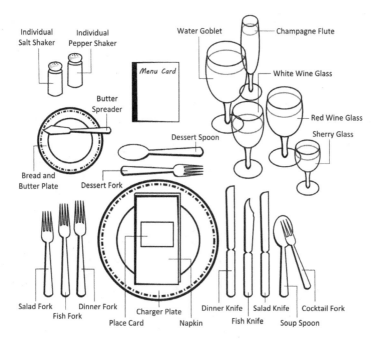

Individual Salt Shaker | Individual Pepper Shaker | Water Goblet | Champagne Flute | Menu Card | White Wine Glass | Butter Spreader | Red Wine Glass | Sherry Glass | Dessert Spoon | Bread and Butter Plate | Dessert Fork | Salad Fork | Fish Fork | Dinner Fork | Charger Plate | Place Card | Napkin | Dinner Knife | Fish Knife | Salad Knife | Soup Spoon | Cocktail Fork

The place setting tells you how many courses you'll be having and gives you a general idea of what you'll be eating. Start from the outside in. If you don't know, take it slow. If necessary, implement the monkey-see, monkey-do strategy.

3 The salad fork may be placed on the right side of the dinner fork when the salad is served as the last course (European style).

4 Individual salt and pepper shakers are provided for convenience. You don't have to interrupt anyone to make your request. (Always pass them together as a pair.)

What's Wrong with This Picture?

Can you find all twelve mistakes?

From the left:

Diner A:
> A bit underdressed (A t-shirt? Not a horrible offense, but you could put a little more effort into it.)
>
> Slouchy
>
> Sneak texting

Diner B:
> Standing
>
> Drinking out of the bottle (excessive)
>
> Not sharing

Diner C:
> Napkin is not on his lap.

Diner D:
> "Oh, no, you di'n't" snap at the server
>
> Bad attitude to go with that "snap"

Diner E:

Feet on chair

Reclining (You're not at home!)

Napkin not placed correctly

RSVP: *Respondez s'il vous plait*

Next to cell phone rudeness, this is right up there. Why don't people RSVP?

RSVP does not mean "only if you feel like it," "when you know for sure that nothing better pops up," or "after you've seen the guest list and menu."

Not replying will earn you a poor reputation—unreliable, apathetic, and inconsiderate.

If you don't want to go or you have a prior commitment, reply immediately.

If your attendance is mandatory, reply immediately.

If it's beneficial for your career, reply immediately.

Reply within the given time.

If you forget to reply on time, don't dismiss it. Reply along with an apology.

By the way, it's time to drop the high school "I'll go if you go" routine.

....

KEYS FOR REMARKABLE BUSINESS DINING MANNERS

"The way you cut your meat reflects the way you live."—Confucius

- Arrive on time. (If you are unfamiliar with the meeting place, start off early.)
- Dress appropriately. (If the restaurant is upscale, put on a jacket and real shoes.)
- Do not place your purse, keys, or briefcase on the table.
- Put away your cell phone! (No photos of your Niçoise salad are necessary.)
- Leave your shoes on. (Yes, I really had to include this!)
- Don't move around the place setting because you need space for your stuff or your elbows.
- Don't take over the conversation (even if you think you are the most interesting one at the table).
- Pace yourself. (Yes, you can!)
- Don't request a doggy bag. (It's just not professional to walk out with a cardboard box as you shake hands.)
- Don't whip out the dental floss or use your toothpick or pinky nail to remove the stuck piece of

broccoli while you're at the table.

- Swallow before sipping.

- Don't swoosh your finger around your mouth to get the leftover chunks. (That's super gross!)

- Prepare general, upbeat topics for conversation. (For example, books, movies, new food you've tried, hobbies, upcoming vacations, new fashion trends, positive workplace trends, etc. It will go over well with your boss or coworker.)

- Take small bites, and chew with your mouth closed, please.

- Don't cut up all of your food at once—one piece at a time. (Looks like mush, and ready for a two-year-old to dig in.)

- Don't lecture anyone about diets, why everyone should be a vegan, the lousy menu selection, war, religion, or politics. (Let's stick to less explosive topics. "Have any of you seen [insert the latest reality show]?")

- Don't use ice cubes to cool your soup. Don't blow on it. (With your spoon, skim from the top away from your body.)

- Don't wave your knife or fork around (unless you're Italian).

- Use your napkin regularly—especially if you have a mustache or a beard.

- Don't snap your fingers at the servers or try to be cool by yelling out "*Garçon!*"

- Always use "please" and "thank you" when you

speak to the server. (A condescending tone lets your arrogance come shining through.)

- Your posture is a reflection of your state of mind. (Slouching = I'm bored, tired, or just plain apathetic. Sit up straight; you can do it!)

- A burp of satisfaction is never acceptable. If one slips out, cover your mouth and, in a low voice, say, "Please, pardon me."

- Don't reach across the table. Ask for it. (Don't interrupt a conversation over it; wait.)

- When you don't know which fork to pick up or how to eat escargot, pick a person at your table who "looks" like they know what they're doing and follow them. Hey, at least you won't be embarrassed alone.

- If the conversation is heating up, don't encourage it; just stop talking.

- If you eat too fast, put the fork down after every bite and don't pick it up until you've swallowed.

- Don't grunt and announce that you're stuffed.

- Don't lick your utensils or your fingers. Ever!

- Don't ask if you can "try some" from someone's plate. (Maybe if you were on a romantic date.)

- If you see a beetle or a human hair in your risotto, quietly call the server over and tell him/her. (Don't make a huge scene or post about it on social media; it happens.)

- Avoid alcohol. (None is preferable; limit yourself to one, and not a double.)

- Do not ask for more food, dessert, drinks . . . especially when everyone else is finished. (Reminder: business meals are not about the food; they are about building a relationship and learning.)
- Please don't pocket sugar packets or anything else that isn't bolted down.
- Don't complain.

Dining etiquette comes down to this: just don't do anything that would gross out the other person or make them question your professionalism.

Lingering Coffee Shop Meetings

First of all, if you've chosen to meet in a coffee shop, I hope you don't require privacy; you don't know who may overhear your conversation, or worse, record it.

- If you stay over an hour or so, tip above what you'd normally tip (you are taking up "new" customer tips.)

- Consider using a note pad and pen to take notes instead of your laptop or notebook. (Old-school, I know, but it takes up less space, avoids the clicking sound, and assures the other person that you aren't checking your emails.)

- Arrive early to secure an out-of-the-way table.

- Order something. It's not a non-profit community center.

Rosalinda Gets Personal:

I met someone at a coffee shop (the kind that serves a real breakfast). Anyway, I presumed that we were having breakfast, at least a pastry or fruit plate and coffee. About fifteen minutes into our meeting, I asked if we should order. He informed me that he wasn't planning on it, and that no one would mind if we just sat without ordering anything. I was flabbergasted. Taking up space affects the server's tips for the day. What did I do? I ordered some food; he still refused, even after I informed him that it would be my treat. If you have financial constraints, meet at an office or park. Even libraries allow you to use their facilities.

To be clear about it, ask the person you are meeting in advance if he or she plans on eating. It's awkward to eat while the other person just sits there. Sheesh!

WORKPLACE CUISINE

Mmm, Mmm, Malodorous.

Stinky foods: the best way to make enemies of your coworkers. And don't forget about the client who walks in; will the smell affect his or her attitude toward you? Your product? Your company?

Potent smells can trigger bad moods. Here are some of the foods people find most odoriferous: any kind of fish, onions, dishes with full-bodied cheeses, curry (sorry), green veggies, hard-boiled eggs, and, an all-time fav', microwave popcorn (it lingers).

The scent of any food or snack can set you off or cause

distraction. Being considerate of those you work with is just plain good manners.

Equally distracting is the sound of someone opening a bag of their favorite chips and crunching and munching to their heart's delight. And the sound of fingers being licked can be revolting. While you are in the solitude of your cubicle, enjoying your crunchy treat, your neighbor is probably daydreaming about how they'd like to grab the chip bag, toss it in the trash, and spray the area with some gardenia-scented product.

So what is the answer? A poster listing certain aromatic foods as off limits? Who decides what's acceptable or not? Would anyone adhere to the rules?

"Troy, would you like some? I made it myself?"
(Troy: Plugging your nose? Not nice or necessary.)

> ### Consider this:
>
> If you must enjoy a loud or pungent culinary delight, at least go to the lunchroom or take it outside. Another option is to enjoy your tasty treat on the way home. When eating at your desk, use some grace and discretion. Use the same manners you'd use dining at a restaurant.
>
> - Take small bites.
> - Use a napkin. (Wash your hands afterward; handing someone the agenda with orange fingerprints is a little gross.)
> - Don't lick your fingers.

Lunchroom Plunderers

It is unbelievable to me that an adult would take something that does not belong to them! It's like the lunch-money bully at school. At least he/she had the guts to ask for it face to face.

Short of installing a hidden camera inside the lunchroom fridge, it is difficult to catch the food thief.

> ### Dear Lunch Room Food Thieves,
>
> If you can't afford groceries, maybe you should evaluate your expenses. Cut out cable. If you're just too lazy to make a trip to the grocery store, sign up for a delivery service. If you're always running late and forget to grab a snack from home, buy something on your break. Just stop stealing other people's food! Thank you.

Ideas to discourage the lunch room plunderer:

Bring it up at the next meeting (not sure what good that will do, but . . .)

Bring your lunch in a cosmetic type bag with a lock on it.

When you brown-bag it, staple it.

Place a note inside your lunch bag, "You don't want me going hungry, do you?"

Basic Lunchroom Behavior

Refrigerator: Label your food, throw it out before it grows fuzz, don't take it if you didn't make it, wipe it if you spill it, and refill it if you emptied it.

Conversation: Keep it down, keep it PG-13 (or even PG), include others, read a book if you don't want to talk, and keep your intrusive phone call to yourself.

Eating: Avoid aromatic foods, clean up after yourself, practice basic table manners (you aren't at home), and don't be a mooch.

Space: Don't put your feet up, don't spread your stuff across the table, don't move someone's lunch bag because they're in "your spot".

Email to All Staff—Subject: Surprise Treats in the Lunchroom

Donuts, bagels, Chinese takeout—whatever it is, take only one serving and only while you are at work!

When your company is generous with you, don't take advantage of it or complain.

The "Taker's" Attitude:

- "Awesome! I'm takin' some for dinner tonight."
- "They don't pay me enough; I'm taking what I can get."

- "Geez, is this the best they can do?"
- "Finally! They need to do this more often."
- "I hope there's enough, 'cause I'm starving.

Doesn't that sound ungrateful?

Rosalinda Gets Personal:

I was meeting a client who asked that I wait for him in the company lunchroom. As I waited, an employee quietly entered. Naturally, I looked up. We made eye contact for only a split second; she was on a mission. She pulled out a few plastic containers and began to fill them with the company-purchased, catered food, which, by the way, no one had savored yet. I was in disbelief, but it was not my place to say anything. In addition, things aren't always what they seem. After hurriedly stuffing her containers, she stacked them in an orange reusable bag, and with a lowered head, she disappeared. Did I tattle to my client? Yes, but only because he wondered why so much food was already missing. He did not seem surprised when I described the woman. And, no, she wasn't going through tough times. She was just a moocher.

KEY POINTS:

- Brush up on table manners.
- Try to have alternate topics of conversation.
- Avoid or limit drinking during work-related functions.
- The workplace lunchroom is not your home.

- Take small bites.
- Use your napkin.

- RSVP!
- Remove your hat and keep your shoes on.
- Don't take what's not yours (even if it's just a yogurt).

C H A P T E R   9

M A I N L Y   M A L E

> "The integrity of men is to be measured by their conduct, not by their professions."—Junius, pseudonym of a writer for the Public Advertiser

CHIVALROUS ACTS

Many of the men I've spoken with say that they still open the door for a woman, even in the workplace. While most women are not insulted by this gesture, a man must be prepared for the few who might be.

Gentlemen, anticipate that there will be a woman or two who will bite your head off, instead of giving you the more conventional, gracious, and polite response: "Thank you."

Equality in the workplace is extremely important, but has it gone too far when it matters who opens the door? In the workplace, everyone handles their own door or adheres to the "whomever reaches the door first, opens it" policy.

Putting such great emphasis on such a small gesture can put up barriers between people, especially between the sexes. It also creates a tone of pettiness and even disregard for one another, which is detrimental to the atmosphere of any workplace.

Look, gentlemen, I'm sure you open the door for anyone who happens to be around, but if you run into Ms. I'll-Do-Myself, respect her preference, and let her get her own door. If she opens the door for you, just say, "Thank you," and move on.

In essence, if you insist on being chivalrous in the workplace, and your female counterpart is offended by your gesture, say, "I'm sorry," and don't do it again.

Other chivalrous acts you might consider giving up during work hours:

- Pulling out a chair for a woman: Another no-no. Only offer to assist people who seem to need it (pregnant women, men or women in crutches or with an arm cast, etc.—and even then, they might decline your help).

- Helping a woman with her coat: Don't even go there! That's way too personal. (It can be misconstrued as a "date-like" gesture. Uh-oh! Off to sensitivity training again.)

- Paying the check: The person who extended the invitation should pay, regardless of gender. That's just common sense.
- Giving gifts: First of all, why are you giving her a gift? Is your relationship familiar enough where you exchange birthday or holiday gifts? Do your coworkers participate, or could they misinterpret this? Is it mutual, or does she feel obligated to exchange gifts?

"Oh, you shouldn't have. . . . Really, you should not have . . . "

- If you exchange gifts with only one or two co-workers, I recommend doing it after work or privately at lunch.
- If you decide to give a gift, keep it generic: coffee, candy, a gift card to a local sandwich shop or bookstore. Avoid anything strictly "feminine."
- Complimenting a female (or even male) coworker: Avoid it for the most part—especially if it's

about her appearance, specifically body parts. If your relationship is more familiar, a general comment (without any grunts, whistles, or alluring gazes) may be fine. If someone goes to great lengths to look smart or has a new hairdo, a compliment is usually quite welcome. Just be sure you don't overstep the boundaries of your relationship. It's all in the delivery.

The Guessing Gay Guy

From the Audience:

Q: Being a gay man, I find that some of the straight men shy away from me. I don't always get asked to join them for after-work drinks. How do I break the barrier without getting in their face about it?—Jacinto

A: Dear Jacinto,

First of all, did you ever stop to think that maybe it has nothing to do with your being gay? Maybe they made plans when you weren't around.

It seems that you are making assumptions with nothing to support your theory. This may have affected your demeanor, and maybe that's why they are shying away from you. Could they be getting the vibe that you are reserved, self-conscious, high maintenance, or even disinterested? Hence, the lack of invitation.

Next time you hear the group talking about going out, smile and go with the flow. Until someone makes a disparaging remark or backs out because you're going, don't get dramatic or assume it's because you're gay.

This is for everyone; your personal life preferences really have no bearing on your job or duties unless you make them. You are there to be civil to everyone and do the job you're getting paid to do.

....

GUY TALK

Because of today's laws and company policies—and with the progression and evolution of society—"guy talk" is not as prevalent in the workplace. With women working side-by-side with men on construction sites, in firehouses, and on many other traditionally male jobs, men have had to curtail their "guy talk."

Whether you are surrounded by men, women, or both at your place of work, the real reason to avoid "guy talk" is that it is unprofessional. Gentlemen, if you still insist on cock-a-doodle-dooing about your romantic conquests, cussin', talking about female coworkers' physical attributes, or mouthing off a bunch of gross stuff, stop—look—assess. Is the group enjoying your conversation topic? How can you tell?

- Do they participate? (Are they sharing too?)
- Do they laugh (not just the perfunctory, nervous kind of laugh)?
- Do they ask follow-up questions (huge clue)?
- Are they looking away (squirming, looking behind their back, or backing away from you)?

Guys don't typically warn or scold another guy; they just distance themselves from that person or keep the relationship on a casual level—but your reputation stays with them.

Reserve the "guy talk" for your friends, if they're into it. Don't be surprised if some of them grow out of it too.

Beware: Speaking about certain topics in "mixed company" (old-school term) can lead to disciplinary consequences if someone finds your topics offensive. Sexual harassment is a quick way to lose your coworkers' respect and maybe even your job.

"What about some of the women . . . I've heard some of them use words and talk about stuff that would make a guy blush!" True, it isn't all that uncommon for today's woman to "guy talk" with the best of them. To each, his (or her) own. It comes down to how you want the world to see you. I encourage everyone to be prudent, especially in the workplace. Useful tip: If the conversation gets too steamy, just walk away.

From the Audience:

Q: I'm attending a trade school. Some of us get together after class for dinner or a cup of coffee. There are a couple of girls in the group, which is cool . . . except when we go out. Every time we've gone out, these women really embarrass us. They get really loud and obnoxious, cussing and yelling at the waiter. And it's not just because they are women. We'd be embarrassed if a man acted that way too. What should we do? —Chad

A: Dear Chad,

Go out to a movie instead! Here is my take on this sticky situation:

Although more common, people still don't typically think of "girls" and "trade school" at the same time. Maybe these women think that if they act the way they think guys act (stereotyping), they'll fit in and you'll accept them. Here are some options to consider:

- After a few more outings, you can hope they see how you gentlemen behave and start to tone it down. (This requires patience with no guarantees.)
- Go to a place that has a quiet atmosphere. (Again, there's no guarantee they'll tone it down.)
- You can have a friendly chat with them. Explain that you don't want to give the school a bad name and that you're trying to adopt a more professional image, etc. (They might tone it down after that. However, they might make fun of you or get mad and refuse to join you in the future. Either way, problem solved.)
- Ignore them. Move to another table. When they ask, simply say that you were trying to have a conversation and they were being too loud.

Cover Your Ears, Little Lady

Please avoid saying things like these to a female coworker (or your girlfriend):

- You wouldn't understand; this is guy stuff.
- Why don't we talk about something you're interested in . . . tell me about your new hair stylist.
  (Actually, this is pretty darn important to wom-
  en. Just don't ask in a condescending tone, or like
  it's the only thing they talk about.)
- I'm sure this wouldn't interest you; women don't
  usually get it.
- Your delicate ears really shouldn't hear this. (If
  that's true, then you shouldn't be saying it.)
- When we start talking about curtains and reci-
  pes, we'll let you know. (You are really asking for
  it now.)

You get the point. When it comes to conversation, keep
it neutral. Don't assume your female counterpart wants to
talk about the new fall color trends or latest chick-flicks.
Also, don't start with the stereotypical "guy talk." (This can
be equally unwelcome.) To avoid tarnishing your reputation,
keep it respectful and professional. There are a lot of things to
talk about that won't land you in HR. Be creative.

Minor Adjustments

Please don't "adjust" yourself in public. (Apparently, this
doesn't apply if you play baseball.)

From the Audience:

Q: At a recent visit to a hair salon, I was seated in the waiting
area when my stylist, Mr. Fussypants, appeared. He stopped

to chat with another client. During the conversation, Mr. Fussypants grabbed his "business"—with gusto, I might add—apparently making a much-needed readjustment (gross and awkward!). I wanted to walk out. —Cami

A: Dear Cami,

Not to diminish the awkwardness of this distasteful deed, he may have been unaware of his habit. Moreover, I would bet that if this deed was brought to his attention, he would be embarrassed.

Also, if the distasteful deed was done with intent to allure, that is an entirely different situation. As you present it, it was not the case.

You did have several choices, however.

You certainly could have walked out. You could have spoken to Mr. Fussypants about it. You could have spoken to the salon manager. You could have requested another stylist. You could have asked Mr. Fussypants to wash his hands. You could have continued with this appointment, never to return again. You could, for future appointments, face the window until you're called.

Gentleman, from time to time, everyone needs to readjust a thing or two; please take it to the restroom or let the itch pass.

Manly Voice

In a professional setting, everyone's voice should be lower, even in the lunchroom. Resounding voices cause distractions down the hall.

I'm not suggesting you whisper or lose your manhood, just remember that you aren't in a stadium.

P.S. Women need to mindful of this too. I'm just keepin' it real.

....

WHAT DOES YOUR LOOK SAY?

> "Don't judge a book by its cover."–George Eliot (Mary Ann Evans), English novelist

This quote is a nice sentiment, but it's not reality. Within a few seconds of seeing someone, we instinctively form an opinion about them. Sometimes there's an opportunity to find out whether our perception matches or clashes with our opinion. If not, we walk away with that opinion forever.

Does your "look" clearly and correctly represent you? Your attitude? Your capabilities? Your career goals?

Grooming and Attire

Comfort, comfort, comfort. It seems that the suit and tie that men wore for years is no longer comfortable. Regular shoes are no longer comfortable, nor is a belt.

Making a few minor adjustments can lead to job security and promotions. A more mature or put-together look for work will make a difference—not only in how you feel about yourself, but also in the way others treat you.

"I decided to start dressing a little nicer for work. . . . I feel more confident and even more capable. People have been treating me differently . . . talking to me more and asking for my opinion."—Greg

Look'n good.

Here are just a few basics to consider:

- Trim facial hair.
- Keep your fingernails clean.
- Nose rings (and earrings) are for weekend wear (in most cases).
- Lucky tennis shoes and flip-flops should remain at home. (If you must expose your toes, please trim and tidy up the toenail gunk.)
- Have fresh breath.
- Depending on company culture, do not overexpose tattoos or wear heavy cologne.
- No "Rico Suave" shimmering shirt, unbuttoned just so, and so tight that your guns are bursting through.

- No picking of teeth or nose or running your fingers through your hair. Crotch adjustment should done in private.

- Remove your hat. If you insist on wearing a hat at work, wear it so that I can see your eyes.

- Keep your pants up, clean, and free from rips and frays.

- Cargo shorts: please don't.
- Tank top: please don't.

Your hair: I get that the whole messy-hair-that-looks-like-I-haven't-washed-it-in-four-days is sexy (well, not to everyone). But looking sexy shouldn't be what you strive for when getting ready for work. Besides, the boss doesn't usually take "sexy" into consideration when review time comes along.

The hoodie craze: It's all good when you're hangin' with your boys, but in the workplace? Besides you're older now; it's time to invest in a jacket, don't you think? You think a client or pretty coworker wants to go out for dinner or drinks with you and your hoodie?

The tennis shoe craze: In some cases, it can be cute; it can also scream, "Oh, look at me, I'm a runner, I'm a tennis player, I'm a hiker, they're just cool . . . " Guys, you're all grown up now. Wear real shoes, once in a while. Of course, if you work at a sporting goods store, pro-shop, active wear shop, school, or maybe even children's stores, behind the counter of a deli, or in the warehouse, it makes sense.

In the end, let company culture dictate your appearance.

Then again, why not dress a notch above the standard? Be the one to bring back a little style and charisma to the workplace.

> "Clean shirt, new shoes
> Silk suit, black tie
> 'Cause every girl's crazy
> 'Bout a sharp-dressed man."—F. Beard, J. Hill, B. Gibbons, members of American band ZZ Top

KEY POINTS:

- Keep workplace conversations and gestures PG-rated.
- Chivalry is nice in social settings; tone it down in the workplace. Keep it gender-neutral.
- Do you have a career goal? Is it clear to management?
- Looking sharp will set you apart, and outsiders will take you more seriously.

CHAPTER 10

FEMALE FOCUS

Whether you hold an entry-level job or the highest ranking position in the company, building and maintaining your professional reputation is a common objective. This is no different than for your male counterparts.

Women all have different reasons for working, as well as different goals. I knew a very capable woman who was offered a promotion every year. And every year, she turned it down. Naturally, she received unsolicited opinions and peculiar reactions from her colleagues. Are you wondering why she turned it down?

She did not want the additional responsibilities. She did not want the additional hours and potential travel. She did not want the additional meetings. The position she held allowed her to preserve her personal life, and that was her priority and goal.

Whatever your position, whatever your reason, whatever your goal, do it with dignity and integrity, and say it with tact and courtesy.

....

TWO CAMPS OF THOUGHT

I find that women are separated into two camps: the work-outside-the-home woman and the stay-at-home (still working) woman.

During the years that I stayed home to be a mom and wife, I received the most grief, diminishing and patronizing remarks, and was even dismissed as someone who couldn't possibly have anything of interest to talk about. Can you guess by whom?

From Mom to Manager

From the Audience:

Q: I knew leaving my child at day care and returning to work would be a difficult transition. It is, however, worse than I anticipated. I cry, I receive regular texts and photos from the babysitter, which takes my concentration away from my work and staff. I can't quit, but I can't go on like this. My boss, who has been very understanding up until now, recently conveyed to me that I have started falling short on some of my tasks. And, I've notice a change in attitude from some of my colleagues. I'm not sure what to do. —Libby

A: Dear Libby,

My heart sincerely aches for you. Leaving your child with someone and walking away is one of the most agonizing moments, ever. I had to do it myself at one point.

Now for the pragmatic response. In most cases, colleagues are a supportive bunch. However, when it begins to affect them or their ability to conduct business as usual, patience and understanding begins to fade. Understandably so.

A personal concern should not affect our work. But, because we are human and have feelings, etc., it does. That is when self-discipline comes in.

Options to consider:

- At the next staff meeting, as briefly and coolly as possible, apologize for your temporary lapse and thank them for their understanding and for pitching in for you.
- Use your break time to text, call, and video chat with the babysitter.
- When/if you become teary, close your office door, visit the ladies' room, or step outside for some fresh air. (Keep a mini-makeup kit in your drawer to touch up.)
- Avoid a droopy disposition (difficult, but you can do it).
- Avoid constantly talking about how much you miss your child or wish you could be home with him or her.
- Avoid exposing colleagues to endless slide shows.

(This is a quick way to lose authority.)

- Avoid devoting every spot on your office or cubicle wall to your child.

- Be sure to show interest in your staff and colleagues.

The Purse Hook | Professional or Prissy?

Should a woman use a "purse hook" at a business dinner meeting? I'd say so. It's much better than placing your purse on the table—you'll see why.

In a professional setting, consider a simple handbag over a huge carryall . . . unless the huge carryall is more of a briefcase style. Also, occasionally purge the purse; toss out the crumpled up coupons, receipts, and half-eaten chocolate bar. Pulling out a pen covered in chocolate—not the most professional look.

- If there is a chair available next to you, place your purse, handbag, or clutch on the seat of the chair.

- If your purse has a strap, you can hang it on the back of the chair (unless it's the size of an overnight bag and it sticks out into the aisle).

- If you use a purse hook, be sure that it isn't glitzy and glam; use a sleek and subtle hook—it should look professional and understated.

- If you use a briefcase-type carry-all bag, keep your lipstick, tissues, keys and wallet in it too; there's no need for a purse.

- If you are seated in a booth, problem solved.

Arguments in favor of the purse hook: In addition to the above options, your purse should not cause the server to trip, spilling the bowl of scalding soup all over your boss or potential client. Further, your dining companions should not be forced to kick it out of the way or trip on it as they excuse themselves from the table. I vote "yes" for the purse hook.

> Initial Washroom Hygiene, one of the UK's leading hygiene and washroom service companies, conducted a study on bacteria on women's purses. They found that "the handles of women's handbags are home to more bacteria than the average toilet flush." [13]

Moreover, in a business setting, I would prefer to quickly retrieve the necessary item from my purse next to me, rather than having to bend down and fumble, returning to an upright position, red-faced, with my hair tossed about.

One final argument in favor of the purse hook: You might want to reconsider placing your purse on the floor for sanitary considerations. Germs and bacteria are imbedded in the restaurant carpet by the shoes of customer after customer— that's just gross.

> Did you know? In 1920, a purse hook was used by Queen Elizabeth II. In the sixteenth century, men, women, and children carried purses—until the dawn of pockets. [14]

Reduce the risk: Instead of slinging your bag on the floor, hang it on a hook whenever possible—especially in public bathrooms—and keep your bag off the kitchen counter. Also, use disinfectant wipes inside and outside of your purse.

Powerful Penelope

From the Audience:

Q: I want to be seen as a strong and empowered woman in the workplace; how do I do that without coming across as too masculine?—Penelope

A: Dear Penelope,

Without knowing what you are doing or saying that would cause anyone to consider you to be masculine, I can only provide you with the following suggestions:

- Don't hang out only with male coworkers.
- Don't feel as though you need to dress like a man; you're not one.
- Don't order a bourbon on the rocks just because you think it's manly. (If that's your favorite drink, bottoms up.)

- Don't alter your natural speaking voice, inflection, or use verbiage you deem masculine.
- Don't smoke a cigar just to fit in.

- Don't throw your feet on top of your desk, especially if you are wearing a dress. (Men shouldn't do this either. It's unprofessional.)

> "Successful people understand that you don't need to make things complicated."—Anne McKevit, TV personality and entrepreneur

An earnest and proficient woman doesn't need to prove it. Just allow courtesy, consideration, respect, and tact to guide your words and actions. Build confidence by doing your job well and by getting along with others.

Feeling Alone

From the Audience:

Q: I have always had a strong personality. I know what I want, and I ask for it. To me, revealing any sign of sensitivity, nurturing, or using an amiable tone at work will only breed diminished respect from my staff and colleagues. I feel that I must maintain a stern deportment. However, I am at an impasse; I am a dying breed. This type of thinking or style is not embraced nor practiced by my female counterparts. I don't know how to make the transition to a kinder, gentler attitude.—Alma

A: Dear Alma,

You are correct in your observation. In most industries today, relationships between rank and file have evolved into a more collaborative and receptive approach—not to mention the ease of formalities, including asserting one's position.

I have to commend you for being so insightful, observant, and considerate; all are exemplary and not-so-common traits. However, the old-school way of asserting power can make those around you feel intimidated, blasé to your overplayed role, or worse, they roll their eyes or grimace at your in-your-face style that doesn't fit in with today's workplace atmosphere.

So, what can you do? You may not like it, but here goes:

Use your femininity. Before you flip out on me, read on. I do not mean that you should wear a lacy bra under a sheer blouse, or that you should bat your eyelashes at every man in the office. Do it with something more powerful: your intuitiveness, your ability to foresee potential obstacles, your power of emotional awareness. Allow those characteristics to serve you well.

Here are a few more tips to keep in mind as a woman in the business world:

- Keep your private life private. (Well, as much as possible.)
- Handle your personal problems discreetly; if necessary, fill in only those who will be affected or need to know.
- Don't feign a "know it all" attitude. Ask. If approached properly, most coworkers are willing to help.
- Do not fall into the office gossip circle.
- Maintain a friendly and gracious demeanor. The impermeable approach will not help you in the long run with either male or female counterparts.
- Treat everyone with the same level of respect, from the janitor to the CEO.
- Show interest in others. Keep it general and not too personal.
- Smile. It's not a female or a male thing, nor is it a sign of weakness.

Trying to fit into a mold doesn't work. Your focus will be on your persona instead of your job. And at the same time, if you insist on using an emphatic style of communication, you will be missing out on the opportunity to become a part of a team.

....

THE ENDURING WOMAN

Enduring (a.k.a. older) women have challenges that their younger counterparts would find remarkably alien to their thinking.

An older woman has to maintain leverage and relevance in the workplace. She must continue to keep up with the latest technology, participate in social media, and keep up with the latest lingo.

In addition, she needs to look contemporary. Like it or not, it is reality; appearance plays a role in the workplace.

WARNING: This might be a touchy subject.

Although it may seem shallow to some, maintaining an up-to-date look is helpful, if not essential. Here are a few things to consider:

- Change your hairstyle occasionally.
- Wear makeup. You don't have to go glam; just a little adds a lot of polish.
- Buy new shoes, occasionally.
- Wear a touch of the latest color trend.

- Be aware of the latest movies or trends.
- Engage in an activity, club, or hobby. (This not only keeps you active, but interesting too.)

Younger counterparts, here are a few tips for you to consider:

- Be wise enough to watch and learn from the more experienced women around you.
- Learn to speak and dress appropriately for the workplace.
- Put away your tech gadgets long enough to hold a conversation.
- Open your minds and listen to their ideas. With all the new developments, there are still tried-and-true methods to consider.
- Eventually, your youthful glow will diminish; don't rely on it. Develop your skills, and focus on building a professional reputation. (I warned you it was touchy.)

Insight from an "Enduring Woman": An Interview with My Mom, Dirce

After being home for several years, she returned to work—same industry, but with a few more years to her name.

R: What made you persevere when you felt like you were treated like an "old woman"?

D: I had to prove that I could do it.

R: How?

D: By gaining their respect. I tried to be a step ahead.

I proposed changes. I freely shared (suggested) my expertise with them, without flaunting it in their faces. I was always respectful.

R: Did you feel like they accepted you or took you seriously?

D: At first, they dismissed my ideas or treated them like a joke. I overheard someone say, "She's not going anywhere." And comments like, "She needs this job; who else would hire her?" would hurt, but they also made me stronger and more determined.

R: Not everyone could swallow that and feel motivated to go on. Did you ever say anything to them or to the HR department?

D: You mean did I scream "age discrimination"? No, never. That would only feed into what they thought of me. And besides, what for? Developing mutual respect would be more productive.

R: Wow, what patience and dignity! I guess earning it without running to anyone for help would, in the end, taste very sweet.

D: I allowed my knowledge and experience to show through . . . I continued to share it with them, and then, one day, they realized that I did know what I was talking about.

R: What about your boss; did he acknowledge your worth?

D: Yes, he hired me because of my experience. My goal was to make my boss look good.

I believe that you should learn about and approach your boss's "problems" or "pet-peeves," and solve them for him; prove yourself to be a valuable employee.

R: Do you have any more tips for older people who are returning to work or who work with younger coworkers?

D: Yes. Number one, I always dressed according to my position. Even if I was "in the back," I always presented myself well. Being well-dressed set me apart from the others.

Two, show enthusiasm! Don't complain of pains or limitations. This attitude will pass on to the other employees. How could they work any less than this "old" woman?

Three, sometimes I had to correct someone, but I did it with a solution in mind. We did it together. This elevates the company.

Four, I might have made less money for my age, but why get mad and talk and talk about it? Find out if anything can be done, or when, and either leave or accept it.

Five, it helps to have a sense of humor. Comments will come and go. It is important how you handle them. Most times, they aren't personal. It also breaks the stereotype that older people don't know how to have fun.

R: Were there any other awkward moments or something that stands out in your mind?

D: I remember that an African American guy, who was also in a management position, approached me privately to say, "We have to help each other." . . . I didn't know what he meant. He said, "Look at the color of our skin . . . " First of all, I am very fair, but I got his point. Because I had an accent, I was obviously foreign, so he felt we were "minorities" together. I looked at him and said, "Forget that! Look at my age. I've paid my dues. Besides, I don't care where you came from, we are here to work."

R: So, in essence, work hard, work harder, and prove it. I like it! And by the way, thank you and Papa for demonstrating and instilling that philosophy in me. I instilled it in your grandsons too.

> "Age is something that doesn't matter, unless you are a cheese."—Billie Burke, actress

Do it with dignity:

- Do not use intimidation to get what you want.
- Earn respect; don't demand it because of rank, age, color, gender, etc.
- Be amiable and approachable.
- Be of service to others.
- If you have preconceptions about a superior or coworker, drop them. Take time to find out who the person is on your own terms.

- Don't succumb to gossip or hearsay; it may impede you from an opportunity to explore and develop a mutually rewarding relationship.
- Listen. Percolate. Respond.

Would you like to go to my belly dancing class with me tonight?

....

ATTIRE: BUSINESS VS. WEEKEND

Ladies, if you don't want unseemly attention, you might want to consider leaving the following apparel as weekend wear. (Again, it depends on your career field.):

- Leggings/jeggings/skinny jeans* and fishnet/camo/psychedelic-colored stockings (*Can be suitable if toned-down with professional blouse.)

- Shorts
- Ripped or embellished jeans (Dark wash can be suitable.)
- Huge hoop earrings (a safety hazard)
- Backless, halter, cami, low-cut, and see-through tops
- Super-sparkly anything
- Childhood caricatures (Well, maybe if you work at a preschool or ice cream shop.)
- Short skirts/dresses
- Tennis shoes, flip-flops, heels so high that you can't walk without holding on to a wall, house slippers (yeah, I really had to include this one), and stripper boots

Let them focus on you. Attract honorable, deserved, merited attention with your work and your skills. Don't let your booty shorts do the talkin', because they might be saying something you don't mean.

Ladies, I'm all for femininity. You don't have to go extreme and wear only masculine, tailored gray, black, and navy suits with sensible shoes. Try to balance it; if you wear semi-sexy pumps, keep everything else low-key. One or two "feminine" items balances the look.

Use common sense. If you work in a factory environment, naturally, jeans will be appropriate, as will tennis shoes. No matter what the dress code is, wear it well, wear it clean, wear it professionally, and then take it up a notch.

To Hose or Not to Hose

From the Audience:

Q: Is hosiery out? Should one go bare-legged, regardless of the condition of the leg (visible veins, aging, etc.)? Can I wear black nylons? What about tights? Can I get away with bare legs during the summer months?—Collette

A: Dear Collette,

Wearing hosiery creates a more polished look. There are certain industries or professions that wearing hose is advisable, if not strongly encouraged. For example, hospitality, legal, finance, some government jobs, and perhaps at upscale boutiques.

If the skirt or dress is described as a suit, then hose should be considered. There are regional considerations as well. During the hot and humid summer months, you may choose to leave the silky accessory in your drawer.

As to the "condition" of a woman's legs: if your legs are unblemished and you don't have visible tattoos (company's viewpoint) or protruding veins, you may be able to get away with bare legs. Or, you can choose to throw caution to the wind and go bare-legged anyway. Think of pantyhose as a little blush for your legs.

Keep the hosiery color neutral. If the tights have a design, keep the rest of your outfit understated. Fishnet stockings? Probably not in a conservative environment.

Additional considerations: No flip-flops, super strappy sandals, or glittery-kitten heels, of course. If you are exposing your tootsies, be sure that you've cleaned the goo from under your toenails and your polish isn't chipped away. In most cases, rhinestone-gilded toe nails are for weekend wear. You want to avoid sending a "come hither" message to your coworkers.

Check your company's policies and procedures manual. Are you striving for a management position? Do you want to be taken more seriously? Will this image enhance your professional presence? Be the one to raise the bar when it comes to professional attire.

I Don't Need No Stinkin' Makeup!

Surveys (take them or leave them) indicate that women who wear makeup earn more than their au natural counterparts. Women who add a little foundation or powder and lipstick give the impression that they are put together and polished.

During a presentation, a woman in the audience stated that she was adamantly against wearing any makeup. She expressed that she "didn't need it." (I'll implement tact and keep my opinion to myself.)

"By all means," I said, "you are certainly free to choose what is best for you and your image" (politely cheeky).

I wish I could have continued the conversation to learn why women are so opposed to makeup. Since then, I've come up with a few thoughts of my own:

- It's fake. (Do you color your hair? Do you use tanning lotions? Do you polish your nails? Hmm?)
- I don't have the time. (Yes, you do; you just don't want to spend it on this.)

- I don't want to spend money on it. (How often do you really buy makeup, anyway? It's a once or twice a year investment—cut out a latte or two.)
- I look fine. (Perhaps, but do you look your best?)
- Men don't have to wear it. (I beg to differ; although they don't "have to," some do have a beauty regimen.)
- I have sensitive skin. (Problem solved! There are oodles of natural products available!)
- On principle . . . I find it sexist. (Why? Men and women are different, and our society, as a whole, has decided that a woman looks more put together and professional with a little makeup. You and I know that lipstick has nothing to do with a women's abilities. It's like combing your hair, matching your clothes, having clean fingernails, or putting on a piece of jewelry. All of these components tell people a little something about you.)

If you are hesitant about how to buy and apply makeup, make a small investment in yourself and approach a makeup counter at a local department store. You aren't covering up; you're enhancing your natural beauty.

CHIVALROUS ACTS UPON YOU

I saw a woman turn to a man who had reached to open the

door and say, "I've got it." Oh, it wasn't the words so much; it was the tone and expression.

Ma'am, with all due respect, I believe the more courteous response would have been, "Thank you."

Would that same woman be miffed if the same obliging act was done by a woman?

In today's workplace, everyone is equal. However, when a person—any person—hands you a "gift" (any kind gesture), shouldn't you accept it graciously?

Most men who "impose" these chivalrous acts upon women are not sending any type of message. I do not believe that they are trying to "keep me in my place" and remind me that, without them, "poor little ol' me wouldn't know what to do with myself." (Southern drawl required here for the full effect.)

Their mama (a woman) taught them to open doors for others, and they probably saw their daddy do it for their mama.

Would you rather they race around you and let the door slam in your face?

If these tradition-based gestures bother you, politely and discreetly say, "Thank you, Bartholomew. I appreciate the gesture, but I prefer to do this myself." Hopefully Bartholomew will remember to wait for you to open the door for him next time. Just playin'.

There are also women who don't mind chivalrous acts. That doesn't make them any less professional or competent.

How it used to be: In the 1920s, it was "the woman's privilege to bow first when meeting men acquaintances. Young unmarried women usually waited to be recognized first by married women." [15]

Q: You're out to lunch with a male client or colleague. Let's say you invited him, so naturally, you expect to pick up the tab. Now, this gentleman grabs the bill insisting he's "got this one." How would you handle it?

A   Grab it from him and sternly explain that you are fully capable of paying.

B   Calmly ask him for it, and when he does not comply, drop it and thank him for the meal.

C   Pull out your credit card and insist on splitting the bill.

The rule of thumb in the workplace is the person who reaches the door first opens it, regardless of gender.

A: The answer is b. Causing a scene is a much worse offense. Struggling for the bill, especially in a business setting, is never recommended. Here's a tip: the next time you invite him (or anyone) for lunch, arrive early, and hand your credit card to your server.

> "Swallowing your pride occasionally will never give you indigestion."
> —Unknown

WOMEN GET PERSONAL

From the Audience:

Q: You say that people shouldn't share a lot of personal information at work. Well, I'm new at a job, and there is no way anyone will get to know me if I keep to myself. I mean, the other women at work have been there longer than me and have their little cliques established. I'd like to know how to make friends with them if I'm not supposed to share personal stuff. I don't want them to think I'm stuck up or a snob or anything like that. If they talk about their personal life, why shouldn't I?—Doris

A: Dear Doris,

First of all, why do you think that unless you spill your guts, you have to keep to yourself? Since you're new, there are always work-related topics to talk about. Secondly, are you upset about the pre-existing cliques or that you have to find a way to form relationships?

Find common ground with a work-related topic, then the conversation will eventually lead to a weekend activity, television shows, or an upcoming family vacation. For the most part, focus the conversation on interests or current events.

Doris, I'm not dictating that you refrain from sharing your life, but I do ask that you consider this:

Is that all you have to talk about? Do you have your family's permission to share personal stuff? Is what you're sharing beneficial to your image?

Women can find a million topics to talk about besides how your boyfriend never makes the bed. We don't necessarily have to share only intimate details to feel connected. Besides, should there really be cliques in the workplace?

After a little sharing, be the one to change the subject to a cheery and general topic of interest; keep it professional and welcoming to all genders.

> Every so often, sit with other people in the lunchroom—including your male counterparts. Leave the high school "popular table" image behind.

From the Audience:

Q: I dress nicely. I like nice clothes, and I know what looks good on me. A lot of the women in my company give me looks and even make comments about what I wear. I know that they are jealous. What can I say to them?—Ingrid

A: Dear Ingrid,

I'm not sure what it is you wish to say to them other than,

"Stop looking at me, and stop talking about me!" which you are free to do. They are free to deny it, roll their eyes at you, and have even more to gossip about, further breeding an antagonistic atmosphere.

With all due respect and with no intention of making assumptions or of insulting you, are you friendly and do you conduct yourself in a professional manner toward these women? Do you look them up and down, turning your nose up at their outfits (without being aware of it, of course)? Do you diva strut around the office? Do you boast about your looks or where you shop?

The fact that you suspect jealousy may affect your attitude toward them. Also, this could be a simple case filled with misconceptions.

If you are cordial, it seems odd that they would shun you, rather than compliment you.

My suggestion is to start saying, "Hello," and asking to join them for coffee or lunch. Get to know them, and let them get to know the woman in the fashionable clothes.

KEY POINTS:

- Don't diminish yourself by believing that the only way to get to know someone is to tell all.

- What you wear sends a message. What message do you want them to get?

- Enhancing your natural beauty takes little time and little effort, but the image you create is big.

- Don't fall into the clique trap.

- Accept your current situation; conduct yourself with dignity until you can change it.

- When you are the recipient of a chivalrous act, accept it graciously. It isn't necessary or professional to chastise the chap.

- Let your skills and competence—not your attitude and clothing—do the talking.

CHAPTER 11

PUPIL TO PROFESSIONAL: AN OVERVIEW FOR NOVICES

Congratulations! You got the job. Now you have to be sure you keep the job beyond the ninety-day probationary period.

Have you decided where you stand on your image, principles, work ethic, and boundaries? Have you considered what effect your words and gestures have on your professional image?

Is your goal to develop a professional reputation or just to get a job and see if "they" work out for you? Do you need this job? Did you take the job until something better comes up? Your answers will affect your attitude.

You may find that a few of the points covered here have already been illustrated in other chapters, but because this portion of the book is devoted to you, the novice employee, it covers significant and relevant aspects that can make your first day on the job, and beyond, phenomenal. Dude, let's get started.

....

OFF TO A
GOOD START

Whether you're an entrepreneur or an employee working for an international company, your attitude, attire, words, and gestures represent and reflect not only you, but also your company.

Communication Checklist:

- Don't call people "dude," "bro," "dawg," or any other names, for that matter. (Avoid pinning nicknames or shortening people's names.)

- Don't use your college nickname at work.
- Avoid using (or overusing) trendy terms: *like, man, cool, awesome, frickin'.* (It's time to leave it behind or for weekend use only. Ya feel me?)

- Swearing, poor grammar, and speaking in incomplete sentences: not profesh. (You want to be taken seriously, right?)

- Listen and learn. Ask questions. And try not to respond, "Yeah, I know," Or "Yeah, I've got it," while nodding impatiently or checking your phone. (This is where a little humility goes a long way—especially if you're dealing with an "experienced" coworker.)

- Keep your phone out of sight (especially in front of your boss). What can be more important than showing him or her that you can focus?

- Don't interrupt (unless the building is on fire).

- Keep your voice under control (especially if you are in a cubicle environment).

- Don't raise your voice. Ever. (If you think you're about to lose it, or there's mass bickering, excuse yourself.)

- Don't walk out just because a conversation doesn't interest you or you didn't get your way. (That's super rude.)

- You don't have to say it just because you think it. (Using tact can keep you from sticking your foot in your mouth.)

- Greet people. "Good morning." (Too old-school for you?) If you make eye contact as you walk past someone, smile and nod. Looking away or ignoring someone sends out a message that you think you're just too awesome to talk to them.

> If you overdo it, "casual and friendly" can quickly evolve into an attitude of indifference and arrogance—two very unattractive and undesirable traits.

Is this already sounding too formal? It isn't; it's professional. Try it. I bet you'll start feeling more confident and maybe even take your job more seriously, not to mention be seen as a leader or influencer (someone who's got it goin' on).

....

CONVERSATION
CONTROL

Topics: Keep it professional. Keep it PG. Keep it gender-neutral. Keep it positive.

By now, you must have the list of conversation topics to avoid memorized. If not, allow me to introduce them to you: politics, religion, sex, unethical behavior, and company bashing. (Wow, what will you talk about?) If you get stuck in the middle of a heated discussion, just listen, don't pick sides, and try to change the subject.

Say something like, "I try to stay away from these topics," or "Let's get back to work." If all else fails, excuse yourself to the restroom or somewhere.

From the Audience:

Q: My colleague (Steve) and I were standing at the door of my office. We were quietly discussing a movie we'd recently seen. We commented specifically about the steamy romantic scenes, mentioning nothing graphic, only how well done it was. Shortly after that conversation, Steve and I were called into HR. Apparently, our coworker "Belinda" had walked by and overheard a portion of our conversation which she found offensive. We immediately apologized to Belinda, but in our minds, we were fuming.

We wished we could say, "Who invited you into the conversation?" "Eavesdropper!" or "Why didn't you just come to us directly with your complaint?"

How should we have handled it?—Derrick

A: Dear Derrick,

Here's the moral of the story: don't talk about what you wouldn't want HR to hear about. At least not while you are in the building.

When you hear someone discussing inappropriate topics in the workplace, no matter how interesting it may be, walk away, change the subject, or clearly state, "I don't feel comfortable talking about this." (That takes courage.)

If you overhear something that's a little off-color, don't be a Belinda. Forget about it, and pretend you never heard it. Or privately speak to him or her as a reminder to use more discretion (saving them a trip to HR).

Most importantly, don't spread it. Just don't. If you're dying to tell someone about it, call your dad or grandma, and get it off your chest.

Gossip

From the Audience:

Q: Is it considered gossip if I tell a new employee about what our boss is like or warn her about coworkers she should watch out for? I just want to save her from confrontation. —Riya

A: Dear Riya,

First of all, how kind of you to want to safeguard the new girl from the treacheries within your department. There is a difference and a fine line between gossiping and an orientation-like background chat.

In brief, ask yourself whether your boss would appreciate having the new girl learn about his or her habits or preferences? If it is a preference and it would save your boss the aggravation and the new girl the embarrassment, then go for it. However, if it is a personal vendetta or animosity you harbor, keep it to yourself.

Things like:

- "Oh my gosh, she is such a drama queen."
- "Don't even try to help him out; he's never grateful."
- "If she asks you for money, be warned . . . she never pays you back." (This is a tricky one—who wouldn't want to be warned?)
- "She's always talking about her kids . . . "
- "He is just rude to everyone; don't bother with him."

You can tell, right? All gossip.

"Whoever gossips to you will gossip about you." –Spanish Proverb

....

THE ROAMING PHONE FIEND

Your fortune cookie says, "You will soon bump into a wall (or ruin someone's day.)"

There you go again, walking down the hall to get to the meeting, with your head hunched over. You might be missing the chance to say "hello" to your colleague; you might force your colleague to jump out of the way because you don't see him; or, you might crush your colleague's glasses because you aren't watching where you're stepping. Now that's just not considerate or smart.

I get it, and I can even kind of, sort of ~~accept~~ put up with it; everyone has their phone attached, at all times. Some jobs may even require it. To make it safe for everyone, would you, could you, please consider these suggestions?

- If you need to make/take a call or text, move to the side.

- Make it short and sweet, and keep your voice down.

- If it isn't work related, ignore it.
- If you're in conversation with a real, live person, ignore it.
- If you're about to walk into a meeting, put it away.

....

WHAT ARE YOU WEARING?

When your coworkers or boss see you in the morning, are your clothes so wrinkled and dirty that they wonder, *Wow, did he work through the night?*

Dress better than they expect you to. How about tucking in your shirt, belting your pants, wearing a sport coat or tailored jacket, choosing a not-so-tight dress, wearing dress shoes . . . not comfortable, you say? And constantly pulling up your pants or pulling down your too-short skirt is comfortable? Just sayin'.

Not sure what to wear? Ask an older family member, look online, or hire an image consultant. Here are some other tips:

- Update and upgrade your look.
- Leave the skinny jeans, flip-flops, message t-shirt, no-sock boat shoes, exaggerated hairdo, tight-sleeved muscle-bulging shirt, yoga pants, and stiletto heels at home.
- Pull out those tongue rings—*eth*pecially if you ju*sth* got one.

Oh, you have a company-issued uniform, so you think you can skip this part because these tips don't pertain to you? (Sorry, they do.)

- Don't let your uniform get nasty, covered in muck of whatever industry you're in.
- Don't wear a stained, torn, or wrinkled uniform (especially in certain fields like medical, food service, or salon/spa).
- Don't wear it oversized, hanging off, or mismatched; this does not look professional and it gives your clients, coworkers, and superiors the impression that you don't care.

Certain industries and start-ups seem to have developed a culture of a floor-to-work wardrobe. That is, if the shirt on the floor doesn't reek, wear it, run your fingers through your hair, slip on some flip-flops, and you're good to go.

However, the majority of the business world still has a standard for what is considered professional dress. It might be to your advantage to invest in at least:

- a jacket (an alternative to your sweatshirt).
- a dress shirt (an alternative to your t-shirt).
- a pair of slacks (an alternative to your cargo shorts).
- a pair of socks (an alternative to bare feet).
- a pair of dress shoes (an alternative to your flip-flops).

Here are a few reasons you might want to rethink your "casually comfortable" style:

It takes the same amount of time and the same number of pieces to look professional.

Adding a tie is icing on the cake.

- What if you get invited to join coworkers (or your boss) for dinner after work at a nice restaurant?

- What if the girl in the finance department asks you to meet for a drink after work? (Would she want to walk in with you?)

- What if your boss needs someone to pick up a client from the airport? Oh, you wouldn't want to go anyway? Well, considering the image your boss just walked away with . . . you won't ever have to. (BTW, that isn't a good thing, at least, not if you want to establish a reputation that you can be counted on.)

- What if there is a meeting or conference? Oh, that's right, you aren't dressed appropriately to represent the company.

- What if people perceive you as apathetic, neglectful, and even unwashed?

- Do the leaders in your company dress like you? (Remember: long-term vision.)

So when you think about your comfort as the most important factor in deciding what to wear, cool, just keep in mind that people outside your department or company are making conclusions about you. And if your attitude still is, "I don't care," all I have to add is, "It's your choice!"

Q: Whom do you dress for?

A: The correct answer is, for the person(s) who decides your career fate.

P.S. Like it or not, we do judge a book by its cover. At least, until we open the book and see how wonderful it is inside. Unfortunately, the cover is all someone has time to see before they make a decision.

> Put on a smile; it's the best accessory, and budget-friendly, too.

TAKING TIME OFF

You just got hired, and you begin to accumulate vacation days after thirty days. Woohoo, Vegas weekend! Dad's timeshare, here I come! Please don't. Take some time to establish yourself within the company. Let your coworkers and boss(es) see that you are dependable before you take your getaway vacation and they realize that you are expendable.

- Unless you have a pre-booked and paid-for holiday (which, of course, you disclosed and received approval for at the time of hire), do not request time off.

- Unless you, your dad, or your child suddenly require surgery, do not request time off.

- Unless someone passes away and you must attend the funeral, do not request time off. (I wouldn't use some distant, twice-removed, third cousin's death as an excuse to take a vacation; your demeanor—lack of sadness—will shine through, as will your tan.)

....

GOPHER! FETCH ME SOME COFFEE, WOULD YA?

- "Make copies of these, and don't forget to staple them this time!"
- "Answer my phone, would ya?"
- "Print these handouts for the meeting."
- "Check with IT to make sure . . . "
- And so on . . .

Think you're too good for these jobs? Would you have trouble doing them with a good attitude and a smile on your face?

"Too many people quit looking for work when they find a job."
—Unknown

If you claim, "It's not in my job description," consider this:

- Are these requests occasional? If so, just do them, gladly.

- Are your efforts recognized? Maybe not at the moment, but at some point? (This is a good thing.)

- Is it because you're the only one your boss can count on to do it right? (This is also a good thing.)

- Are you sure they aren't in your job description? If they aren't, do them anyway, as long as they don't keep you from completing your real duties.

- If these side tasks begin to consume a lot of time, make an appointment with your boss to discuss it.

> Glad you got the job? Let your attitude reflect it.

You are new on the job, learning the ins and outs—the grunt work will only make you more viable, valuable, and visible. Do more than you're expected to do.

TAKE THE RAP; SHARE THE GLORY

When things go well, everyone wants a piece of the glory. But what happens when you encounter a glory-greedy coworker?

You know the person who stands up at the meeting and says things like, "If I hadn't found that report . . . " "I knew I could dig us out of this," "I'm glad I was able to help you guys out," and so on . . . taking a lot or all of the credit.

Instead of jumping out of your chair and shouting, "*WE!* *We* did it! You weren't even there half the time!" and looking like a maniac—maintain your cool, and either let it go, or say something like:

- "That's right, Frank, it took everyone's contribution to make this work."
- "Each of us played an important role in this project . . . great teamwork, everyone."
- "Frank, I'd like to publicly thank you, Marcos, and Stacy for working so well and making sure we got the project done."

Reasons vs. Excuses:

Reasons: Uses facts, judgment, and logic to make a decision or conclusion.

Excuses: Uses pretexts to be released from an obligation or to justify failure or incompetence.

These statements show leadership and acknowledgment of everyone else's contributions, and it shuts Frank up too. (A little shrewd and calculated? Yep.)

Similarly, taking the rap for an unsatisfactory or incomplete task is always the right thing to do—no matter the consequence. Fess up, apologize, and ask how you can fix it.

Please don't bore your boss with a list excuses.

"Well, if only they . . . " "Like, I could have done it if . . . " "If I wasn't so like burned out . . . " "I've been really tired lately." "No one showed me." "Marvelle told me I shouldn't do it like that." (Sure, throw your coworker under the bus.) "I was the only one who . . . " "I had so many other things to do." You get the picture, right?

> "He that is good for making excuses is seldom good for anything else."
> —Benjamin Franklin

CRITICISM:
HOW TO TAKE IT.

No matter how superb you are at your job, eventually someone will criticize you about something—and the criticism may even be unwarranted, which is the hardest to take.

The word *criticize* has a negative, if not aggressive, connotation, which can be the case if it's delivered in a malicious manner.

If we're open to listening, even when the delivery is cruel, we can choose to view it as a helpful tool to improve or change.

From the Audience:

Q: The other day, I was sitting in the lunch room with a couple of coworkers when our boss walked in. She looked right at me and started with, "I've been meaning to talk to you about a few things." She proceeded to recite a list of dissatisfactions: how she'd like me to change how I answer the phone, how I'm not at my desk enough, and how the handouts aren't formatted the way she'd like them to be.

I've been at this job for almost six months now, and she's never said anything to me about any of this stuff, so I was kind of shocked and pretty embarrassed.

Later that day, I asked to speak with her, but she said she was too busy. Nothing's been said since. What do I do?
—Colby

A: Dear Colby,

Well, that was pretty thoughtless and unprofessional of your boss, but that is irrelevant because you can't change her methods.

If not for her timing, her grievances aren't outrageous—nothing you can't handle.

I hope your coworkers were professional enough to keep this little scene amongst themselves. If you are approached by curious coworkers, don't get into it. Merely say, "It's over with," or "We'll work it out." Always stay positive, and don't bash the boss!

Options:

- Schedule an appointment with your boss. Preferably on a slow day, near closing, or whenever she is in a most receptive mood. (You know her best. If you haven't learned her moods, do so ASAP.)

- Make notes to help you remember and keep you on topic. (This can help you from getting emotional—not that you would; it's just precautionary.)

- Thank her for alerting you to her concerns; tell her you appreciate learning about her preferences and improving your skills.

- Politely tell her that it was awkward and embarrassing to be corrected in the lunch room. Explain that you don't want others to get the wrong impression or overhear sensitive information, and that you respectfully suggest meeting once a week to discuss the good and the bad. (Let's hope she realizes her indiscretion and apologizes—don't get exasperated if she doesn't.)

- And finally, you don't have to publicly endure what should be a private conversation. If it happens again, stand up and in a polite tone and calm manner, interrupt, "Excuse me, could we please discuss this privately?"

Confronting Criticism

No one enjoys having someone point out a negative habit or flaw. How we react is what determines whether the situation turns ugly or productive.

If you feel your blood start to boil, I recommend you keep quiet. (If you don't, it won't be pretty.) Don't feel that you must address it right there and then. Taking time to cool off, think, and compose your thoughts can make you come out shining.

Sophomoric Replies to Criticism:

- "That's just the way I am." (Don't be doubly ridiculous by adding, "Take it or leave it." Your boss just might "leave it.")

- "I've always been this way." ("Don't go changin'...")

- "I can't help it; it runs in my family." ("Break the chain, chain, chain.")

- "You're just picking on me!" (Really? You'd use that in the workplace?)

Professional Replies to Criticism:

- "Thank you, I'll take that into consideration." (Even if you don't intend to, say it; it's just polite.)

- "Although, I'm not sure that I agree with you, I do appreciate your remarks."

- "You're the first to bring this to my attention. I'll give it some thought. Thank you."

- "I'm sorry you feel that way. I'll give it some thought and get back to you."

The point here is to respond, not react.

How to Respond Instead of React:

When you've just got to give someone a piece of your mind, ask yourself these three questions first:

1 Is it really necessary?
2 What is my point?
3 How will this help?

(Subliminal message here, said in creepy, ghostly voice:

"Remember your professional reputation . . . professional reputation . . . professional reputation . . . ")

Or don't; go ahead and fly off the handle, and see how that works out for you.

> "Wise men are not always silent, but know when to be." –Unknown

CONVERSATION CUES

Sometimes it's necessary to interrupt a conversation. Whatever you do, don't bellow. Here are six easy steps to avoid interrupting like a first grader:

1   Approach the area where the conversation is taking place.

2   Wait several seconds to allow them to complete their sentence and turn to you. (If they don't acknowledge you, go to step #3.)

3   Wait for a pause, and say, "Please excuse me for interrupting." (Use this phrase with #2, too.)

4   State your case, briefly and quickly. Wait for a response.

5   Upon receiving the information, thank them for their time.

6   Leave. (Do not even think about throwing in a "By the way . . . ")

Unspoken Signals

Looking for unspoken signals can help you determine whether to continue, end, or not even try to begin a conversation. Here are a few signals to be aware of:

- If two people are facing each other and in close proximity of each other, the conversation is probably private. Come back later.

- If two people who are in deep conversation do look up at you, but they don't move, that means say what you came to say, but make it quick and leave.

- If someone is on the phone with their back to you, more than likely they'd like privacy. Come back later.

- If someone stands at the threshold/doorway of their cubicle or office as you begin your conversation and they don't move, that means they want you to keep it brief.

- If someone says, "Sorry, not now; I'll get back to you in a bit," don't respond with, "It's just a quick question." ("Not now" means "not now"!)

- If they keep walking as they spit out the last words, don't run after them.

- Keep your voice at a level that can't be heard in the next department.

- If the person leans back in their chair, looks relaxed, smiles, and has a welcoming tone as they ask you to enter their office, those are agreeable signals—go ahead.

- Know when it's time to end a conversation. Pick up on signals. It is probably time to wrap up the conversation (1) if the person stands up; (2) if the person says something like, "Uh, it was great talking with you," or "Thanks for stopping by"; or (3) if the person looks at the time, stops talking, turns away to check their computer, jiggles their leg, corrects their posture, or suddenly remembers that they need to make a call. Excuse yourself, and make a quick exit.

Learn to pick up on signals. Not everything is or has to be said verbally. Every day, we speak to one another without saying a word.

> Did you know: Folded arms are typically interpreted as "defensive" or "disagreement." According to anthropologists, there are *six* different ways we fold our arms and that we each have a favorite way. [16]

More Conversation Tips

- You might be used to sharing your life with the world through social media; in the workplace, dole it out little by little. Certain things should remain private, including drama-filled problems. Think before you open your mouth; one seemingly insignificant "share" can be a career killer.

- Don't just hang out with coworkers your own

age. Develop relationships with as many people as you can. Learn from the experienced coworkers. This can set you apart as a professional team player and leader. Don't confine yourself in a box.

- Learn to accept criticism with finesse, constructive or otherwise. Sit on it for a day before reacting. Talk it over with a trusted coworker. This is when the "experienced" coworker comes in handy. He or she will hopefully have less emotional or reactive advice.

- Learn to take responsibility if your work was less than satisfactory. No need to throw your coworkers under the bus. Ask how you can do better next time.

- If you are wrong, late, insulting (even unintentionally), interrupted, forgot, or misunderstood, apologize sincerely. That doesn't mean a hasty, "Hey, sorry, man." (Sorry for what?) That style is cool if you're talking with your friends. Upscale it for the workplace; make it professional. Own it: "Laura, I'm sorry for arriving late to the meeting; it won't happen again." (No excuses or blame required.)

Misunderstandings: Trendy Terms in the Workplace

You're young (maybe just at heart). You've got it goin' on. You want to show that you are cool and confident. And you really

No matter how casual the atmosphere in your company may be, there are still time-honored traditions that work well. Your old-school or hip vocab may be okay around your coworkers, but it's not a plus in front of an out-of-town client or at a conference representing the company. Adding a little "corporate style" to your image can't hurt, even if you work on the assembly line or in the warehouse.

want to make sure that you don't develop a corporate-style image.

So, you continue to use the trendy phrases in the work-place—even with your superiors in both rank and age.

Think about how they may react? Will they even understand you? Not only are you reinforcing a casual image, but you may be creating confusion—which leads to mistakes that can take away from the efficiency of your company.

- "Epic" (Are you talking about a novel? Poetry?)
- "My bad." (Nah, you're a pretty nice guy.)
- "Dude, I'm really flowing here." (Hurry, run to the men's room!)
- "Sort of like" (. . . like what?)
- "I'm here 24/7." (Is that a fraction problem?)
- "Dawg" (I love dogs; I have a black lab. And you?)
- "Holla at the celly." (I beg your pardon?)
- "Not a problem." (Glad to hear it. Now get it done!)
- "Can I be honest?" (No, please lie to me.)
- "I know, right?" (Um?)
- "I feel you." (Please don't.)

- "I don't mean to offend you, but . . . " (Well then, don't say it!)
- "I'll be chillaxin' on vacay next week." (I'm sorry to hear that?)

Peace out, spread the love, Dude.

Let's switch it up. Imagine the boss or senior colleague uses phrases like:

- "That's like putting the cart before the horse." (Wha'?)
- "Don't shoot the messenger." (Get down—he's got a gun!)
- "He's not the sharpest tool in the shed." (What's a shed?)
- "She's got ants in her pants." (Is that sexual harassment?)
- "Bless her heart." (Does she have a good cardiologist?)

Imagine how confusing it is for a newcomer or second-language learner if you use words and phrases that not even all first-language speakers will understand.

- "Do I look like I just fell off a turnip truck?" (You weren't wearing your seat belt?)
- "Let's go wet our whistle." (Wait. What?)
- "He's a hard nut to crack." (I'm allergic to nuts.)
- "I'm cool as a cucumber." (Why are you talking about salads right now?)
- "You're running around like a chicken with its head cut off." (PETA! Where's PETA?)

> Did you know? Having "tired blood" was believed to be from sleeping more than your fair share or just plain ol' burn out? Well, here's an English folk remedy to increase circulation that you can try instead of an energy drink; place ants in your pants." [17]

....

CAREER FAIRS

Be prepared. You never know when you might make the contact of your life.

I'm often asked, "Do I have to dress up when I go to a career fair?" In my head I think, *Oh boy, not if you want them to see that this is as good as it gets.*

You do get a pass if there is absolutely no time to change out of your uniform after a big game.

Career Fair Checklist:

- Review the list of organizations that will be present. List them in order of interest.
- Have several copies of your résumé with you.

- Dress appropriately. If you don't know what that means, ask someone you trust. Just remember that it isn't about your comfort; it is about making a good impression and showing them your best. (Guys, this includes wearing real shoes and a belt. Ladies, this excludes date-night outfits.)

- Be prepared to answer basic questions like: What are your interests? What are your goals . . . your skills? Are you willing to relocate?

- Please, please do not ask: How much do you pay? How much vacation time do I get? Do you have an extensive salad bar and on-site barista? Can I bring my dog to work? What does your company do, anyway? What are the benefits? Do I have to dress up? I live kinda far, so I would need flex-time. (Are you kidding me! You are there to impress them, not the other way around.)

- Be prepared to walk alone. This is your life, not

Effort, or lack of it, tells people all they need to know about you.

you and your friends'. Unless they are also interested in the same company, part ways.

- Smile.
- Stay off your phone. (Do your best.)
- Eat before or after the event. Sticky fingers or polish sausage aroma are distracting and gross. By the way, no gum chewing.
- Take the rep's card. (This will help with the thank-you note you will be writing later.)
- It is okay to listen in and participate in an ongoing conversation. You could say something like, "Would you mind if I joined in?" (A mere formality, but shows you are super well-mannered.)
- Thank the company representative for their time.
- Shake hands. (See chapter 1 about how to achieve the perfect handshake.)
- Follow up with the companies that were of interest to you. Send a thank-you note and a brief statement about whatever stood out in the conversation. Consider including your résumé.

From the Audience:

Q: In one of my business classes, we talked about putting on a "hard shell" once we're out in the business world. Being polite and having friendly attitude could be mistaken for weakness. I'm conflicted.—Cyrus

A: Dear Cyrus,

Perhaps there are some industries or occasions where it

would be advantageous to put on a "hard shell." Off the top of my head, the courtroom. In most cases, a courteous and friendly attitude is favorable. You can bet that there will be a wolf or two who will try to take advantage of your amiable demeanor—it doesn't mean you have to accept it or allow it! It is up to you to stand up to them without losing your cool or your dignity and without strong-arming them.

....

EMAIL SENSE REVIEW

One "reply all" can end your career, or at the very least land in you HR for a little chat. By the way, companies can (and do) keep track of workplace communications. This practice is primarily to seek out unsavory and improper content to prevent legal ramifications.

Here are a few tips to help keep your email record proficient and professional:

- If it's personal, don't send it through your work email.
- Don't use the "reply all" unless the sender requests it.
- If the subject changes, start a new email, or change the subject line.
- If you are communicating with only one or two from the mass recipient list, start a new email.
- If you receive a forwarded joke, read it; if harmless (that's a matter of opinion), you can pass it on to a coworker. However, you are on company

> Presume that everything you do, send, or view on the computer is public knowledge. (Yikes!)

time, and your name is now attached to that joke FOREVER. If you don't feel uncomfortable, ask your jokester coworker to remove you from his or her joke list; that way you don't have to read it, forward it, or delete it.

- Reply to emails! Do not ignore it because you don't know, can't decide, or don't feel like answering. The sooner you handle it, the sooner you can move on. A simple "Yes, I can attend," or "No, thank you, I am not available to attend" is enough. Done.

- Be careful how you use the "BCC" function. Use it only for a mass invitation to the company party or a mass email to clients where privacy might be a concern. Don't use it to allow a coworker to see an email and subsequent responses without the knowledge of the other recipients. If you think someone else should be included in an electronic conversation, be aboveboard and explain why.

- If you re-use an email from two months ago, delete the old stuff; check the recipients and the subject line.

- If the topic is of a sensitive nature, make an appointment to speak with the person face-to-face or on the telephone. Telephone or face-to-face is also best for lengthy or detail-oriented communications.

....

DINING TIDBITS

Please note that a few points in this chapter are also covered in the "Dining" chapter.

Being invited to lunch during the interview process is not uncommon. Are you ready to dazzle them at the table? One disgusting or overindulgent move can drown out all of the brilliant conversation. Before you know it, you're back on the job-seeking sites reposting your résumé.

There are pages and pages written on the subject of "business dining etiquette." In this book, I address the basics—enough to get you through the meal without feeling totally awkward. Keep in mind, the meal is not the point; it's the conversation and your conduct.

Tasteless Table Manners

From the Audience:

Q: To help me make a final decision, I typically invite the top three applicants to dinner so that I can get to know them better in a more relaxed atmosphere. Of the final three, only one did not gross me out or baffle me during the meal. If it wasn't a cell phone check, it was details about their bad date, burps, loud grunts of satisfaction after the meal, shoveling food, and the worst, their buddies came up to the table asking us to join them at the bar. The applicant I'd really like to hire lacks basic table manners, but is the most qualified for the job. How can I delicately encourage her to polish her table manners without insulting her? —Jeremy

A: Dear Jeremy,

Easy. Hire an etiquette consultant for your next professional development day. This way, everyone will benefit, including the new hire. Start a new orientation program that includes a business and dining etiquette workshop. Singling her out can be a thorny proposition. She might ask whether you've brought it to the attention of all the applicants/new hires. She can claim you had unreasonable job requirements. You don't want it to become a legal issue.

Before You Dine:

- Arrive on time! Early is even better, even if you have to wait in your car.
- Remain in the waiting area, unless escorted by the restaurant host.
- Do not order or touch anything on the table until your party arrives. (Not even a sip of water.)
- Never, ever arrive starving to death.
- Stand up to greet and shake hands when the others arrive.

Everyone's Here:

- Take your napkin and place it on your lap only

after the host takes his or hers. (After a minute or so, if they don't, take yours anyway.) Do not unfold the napkin entirely; it should remain folded in half.

- Use the napkin regularly, especially if the meal is dripping with sauce. Lift up only the top layer; never bring the whole napkin to your lips.

- Sit up straight. Use your core to hold yourself up. Place your feet flat on the floor in front of you— that helps keep you up. Never lean back in your chair.

Ordering:

- Take the signal from the host. If they order a salad, that's a hint for what price range you should stay in (unless he or she is dieting) and gives you an idea how long the meal will be. (No four-course meal here.) Here are a few foods to avoid ordering: ribs, burgers, drippy sandwiches, spaghetti, or just a cup of soup. Order something equivalent to the host.

- Check out the menu online beforehand. This will save time, and you'll come across as decisive. (Always have a second choice in mind.)

- Avoid alcohol. If the host orders a special bottle of wine to share, you can certainly accept—as long as you are over twenty-one years of age. If you have a drinking problem, it's against your religion, or you hate wine, politely decline. (Don't turn your glass upside down. When the server comes by to pour, place your hand above the glass or say "No thank you"; they'll get it.)

- Be polite and respectful when you speak to the server. How you interact with him or her is a reflection of your character. (Don't be condescending, patronizing, or demanding; that looks very, very bad.)

The Meal:

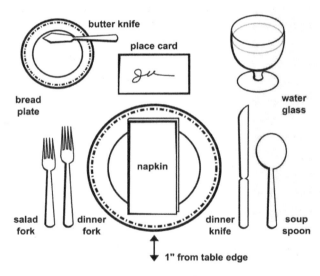

This is a simpler place setting, but many of the same rules apply.

Pick up the utensils from the outside in.

Never switch the place card.

To remember which side your bread plate is on, think: B (bread) M (meal) W (water)

Tips for the perfect meal.

- Wait for everyone to be served before you begin. If your meal is delayed, encourage everyone to begin without you.

- Never snub the server or complain about the meal.

- If the place setting is formal and you have no clue which fork to use, pick someone at the table who looks like they know what they're doing, and copy them. (At least you won't be the only one who picked up the wrong fork.)

- Pace yourself. If you're a fast eater, put the fork down between bites. If you're a slow eater, pick up the pace; you might have to leave food on your plate so that you don't hold everyone else up.)

- Join in the conversation. Don't monopolize the conversation. Don't get personal. Ask questions. Do a lot of listening. (This is where taking small bites comes in handy.)

- If you were invited, you can presume that they are paying. Don't make a scene by opening up your wallet. Just say, "Thank you. The meal was very good." You can add something like, "I'll have to bring my parents here next week." (Don't get too fake about it, though.)

- Unless you are out to eat with familiar coworkers, don't ask for a doggy bag.

- Never bring an uninvited guest.

> "Sneezing will top a hiccup." –Hippocrates, 400 B.C. More sophisticated people suggested spitting on the forefinger of the right hand or crossing the front of the left shoe three times. (Not recommended during a business meeting.) [18]

Hiccups

There you are in the middle of an interview lunch and you get the hiccups.

Options: "I'm sorry...hiccups" (and take a sip of water). If necessary and convenient, you can excuse yourself from the table and find a paper bag, sip water upside-down, ask someone to scare you. . . . Don't apologize after every hiccup; try to carry on as usual.

How many dining goofs can you find?

From left to right: Man #1: fanning mouth; Man #2: slouching, tie undone, possibly texting; Man #3: buttering entire roll at one time; Woman #1: applying lipstick; Woman #2: napkin not on lap, purse on table, and (this one was tricky) spoon placement is incorrect.

Tact, Humility, Respect, Courtesy, Consideration, and Humor

Whenever you speak, put these principles into practice, and you'll soar to the top. At the end of every day, you'll know that you did your best.

Show them that a novice, rookie, millennial, etc. can get it together and contribute positively. Avoid whining, blaming, and excuse-making; no one cares—that, my young friend, is a sign of immaturity (or a sign of your character). Deal with it, apologize, fix it, and move on. Every generation entering the workforce has had to prove itself. You aren't the first, and you won't be the last.

KEY POINTS:

- Avoid gossip.
- Handle criticism with grace.
- You don't know everything. (Sorry to break it to you.)
- Get to know your boss's preferences. Anticipate your boss's needs. Be ready.
- Use discretion when using the company computer.
- A professional look can lead to career opportunities.
- If someone recommended you, you have a duty to protect not only your reputation, but theirs too.
- Don't be too proud to ask for help or too proud to handle a menial task.
- Watch for signals (body language), and take the hint.
- Don't ask what the company can do for you; ask what you can do for the company.
- Adjust to the company culture, and take it (professionalism) one step above—you can't go wrong.
- Use Mr., Ms., Dr.—at least when you first meet someone (and especially during an interview).
- Learn to control your phone addiction.
- Polish your dining skills. (Top Six: chew with

your mouth closed, take small bites, sit up straight, use your napkin, don't burp, and be nice to the server.)

- Before you fall in love, check the company dating policy.

- Upgrade your conversation style; leave the frat house talk behind.

- Sometimes your hunger pains have to wait. (Stuffing your face as you walk down the hall is not a professional look. Besides, you're probably leaving a trail of crumbs behind you.)

- If you're still "livin' la vida loca," use discretion on social media. Be especially careful about posting anything about your job, the company, or your boss.

- Remember, it doesn't always have to be said. In case you haven't noticed, I'm a big fan of "tact."

> "Tact is the ability to close your mouth before someone else wants to."
> —Unknown

CHAPTER 12

UNCOMMONLY COMMON DILEMMAS

Today's workplace is a modern setting with modern attitudes, which typically means there is little desire for formalities. There are benefits and drawbacks to this mindset.

Some benefits include greater collaboration and more open communication between ranks, less money spent on formal business attire, and a less stern environment.

Some drawbacks include the creation of employees who are more prone to share personal problems and feel less pressure to meet deadlines; comfortable clothes can quickly downgrade to sloppy, and an informal communication style may create misunderstandings.

Is the tradeoff worth it? I guess it's up to the company.

Can we attribute the modern "casual attitude" and absence of old-school formalities to the surge of awkward and unconventional dilemmas that were once uncommon in the workplace? Or is the share-all, "my-life-is-an-open-book" philosophy of private life meshing with one's professional life bringing more drama into the workplace?

Whatever it is, these uncommonly common situations can be awkward, time-consuming, unproductive, and so junior high. I hope that your work experiences are pleasant. But in the off chance that an uncommonly common dilemma arises, I'll have provided you with options and general principles that can help ease the awkwardness of the situation.

Hairy Interview Dilemma

From the Audience:

Q: During a recent interview for a sales position, I was following the interviewer down the hall, making our way to the conference room. Along the way, he stopped in one of the cubicles to pick up something. As he emerged, I noticed his toupee was a little lopsided. With the surprise of seeing this, I let out an involuntary snort. He glanced at me without saying a word. The interview proceeded, but my mind was not in it because I was wondering whether I should alert him to his teetering toupee. I did not speak up, nor did I get the job. Should I have said something to him? —Chaz

A: Dear Chaz,

Wow, awkward. I am not familiar with the technicalities

of toupees; however, I do believe that there is a gluing process involved, which, apparently the interviewer did not use enough of.

Not knowing whether a man can feel the piece on his head or not, let's go with a few scenarios.

He may have ignored it because to adjust it would be admitting to wearing a piece.

He may be used to the piece moving about and lives with it. (How would you know that?)

He may have been completely unaware and would have appreciated a discreet word.

Possible reactions: Express appreciation, nonchalantly adjust it and move on, or become super embarrassed making the situation unbearable.

Since you could not focus on the interview because of the topsy-turvy toupee, perhaps taking a chance and speaking up would have been your best option. At some point after the interview, he probably realized it—either by a compassionate coworker or the restroom mirror—and possibly wondered why you didn't say anything.

As a general rule, most people want to be told (discreetly, of course) that something is showing, hanging out, stuck on, or falling off.

Hmm, off the top of my head, everything seems to be in tip-top shape here.

If you think it will help, copy, enlarge, and post this sign in a high-traffic area at work.

....

REENTERING
THE
WORKPLACE

From Skivvies to Slacks

From the Audience:

Q: I've been telecommuting for almost a year. Recently, the company decided to terminate this arrangement. I'm pretty upset about the whole thing, especially because I have commitments. For example, I'm participating in a carpool to get my kids to school . . . I don't know that I would have taken the job had I known the situation would change. —Norris

A: Dear Norris,

Did your employer promise that this arrangement would last forever? Did he or she tell you to incorporate your personal commitments into this arrangement? Did you ask whether this was a permanent perk?

If you answered "no" to the above, you don't have too many options, nor should you really be upset with the company. If this arrangement was presented as a permanent one, make an appointment, get dressed, bring along the paperwork indicating this, and calmly discuss it.

Options to consider:

- You can quit.
- You can apologize to others for your chancy commitments.

- You can quickly make arrangements to fix the problems you initiated.
- Buy new work clothes.
- Speak to your manager to request additional time to resolve matters.

You're Baaaaaack

Returning to the workplace after having worked from home is not only an adjustment for you, but also for your coworkers.

Undoubtedly, there will be one or two of your coworkers who may exhibit a peevish disposition upon your return. How can you win them over?

It is up to you to reenter and reestablish relationships with grace, patience, and effort. Expect a period of adjustment and consider their standpoint:

- They aren't used to having to listen to your opinions or comments throughout the day.
- They may resent you for having been away, not carrying your weight, not attending the endless meetings that they had to endure, etc.; perhaps you are being set up with a newer computer and office furniture or they had to give up space to make room for you.
- They may reply curtly to questions that seem obvious to them.
- They may forget to invite you to lunch or for drinks after work.
- They may become annoyed when you describe

the perks of "a day in the life of working from home."

- They may not cut you any slack.

> Adjust your attitude, attire, and agenda. "A professional is a man who can do his job when he doesn't feel like it; an amateur is one who can't when he does feel like it." —James Agate, British theatre critic.

15 Tips to Make Your Comeback Productive, Pleasurable, and Professional

1 Don't bring your "this-is-how-I've-been-doing-it" attitude.

2 Keep in mind that you are no longer on your own schedule. (That means no streaming your favorite daytime show during work hours.)

3 Act happy to be there. No one wants to hear you moan about how tired you are.

4 Your attire should match your coworkers' attire. (Sorry, no bathrobes.)

5 Your priority should be to meet with each of your colleagues to re-engage.

6 If you aren't sure about something, ask.

7 Listen. Your colleagues can be invaluable in filling you in about rules, protocol, and changes. (This does not include gossip.)

8 If you have brilliant ideas for change, wait a month or so before you present them.

9   You aren't a guest; get up and get it yourself. Don't act helpless.

10 Don't whine about how bad traffic is, how much it's costing you in gas to drive into work, your clothing bill, how you miss watching [insert daytime show] or getting a load of laundry done. (If you do, prepare to see coworkers' eyes roll.)

11 Don't submit a request for "time off" unless it is an emergency. (In your coworkers' minds, you've been on holiday.)

12 Bring in some donuts or a few pizzas for everyone (or healthy stuff if that's what they're into).

13 Most of all, give them time to adjust. (Don't expect their great "enthusiasm" upon your return to last too long. Instead, show your coworkers just how much you will contribute to the workplace now that you are back.)

14 Consider this: If, after a month or so, you are still experiencing discourteous communication or an uncooperative reaction from someone, seek advice from HR.

15 In closing, delight in the fact that you are employed and that you had the privilege to work from home.

....

BIBLE STUDY, DIVORCE SUPPORT, BEAGLE COMPANIONS OF AMERICA, AND OTHER GROUPS

"I'm offended when I walk by the conference room just knowing that there is a religious-type meeting going on in there."

Yes, someone actually said this. My advice is to walk the other way. (Oh, is it out of your way? At least you won't be affected by the dubious assemblage.) Or plug your ears and turn your head away from the closed door when you walk by.

If someone doesn't believe in divorce, should we shut down the support group? If someone is a smoker, should we shut down the Nicotine Anonymous group?

If the company's policy allows people to meet during their lunch hour, then that's that.

Unless the group members are constantly pushing their pamphlets on you, live and let live. Or start your own group. You can name it "The Group against Other Groups (except the ones we approve of)." I'm sure that will make you really popular with your coworkers.

Seriously, will you treat your coworker differently because they gather once a week to discuss religion, the trials of divorce, or the difficulties of breaking the nicotine habit?

Remember what really matters in the workplace. Do they interact with you in a professional manner? Do they perform their duties (which, by the way, is their manager's business, not yours)? What they do on their break should not matter to you at all.

> "Individual commitment to a group effort—that is what makes a team work, a company work, a society work, a civilization work."—Vince Lombardi, American football player and coach.

WHY BEING AN OPEN-BOOK ABOUT EVERYTHING ISN'T ALWAYS JUDICIOUS

Sharing one's viewpoint on subjects like politics, sexual preference/orientation, diet, weight, religion, and child-rearing will happen in the workplace. Discussion of these topics is discouraged for obvious reasons.

If you happen to have a low tolerance level for opposing views and know that you'll pounce on the foe, the key is to resist and retreat. Going off on a tirade will not only not make your point, but you will come across as intolerant, rude, cray-cray, imposing, disrespectful of others, and unprofessional.

Your goal is to maintain composure. And if you can't, excuse yourself before you lose it.

From the Audience:

Q: I recently found out that a colleague whom I've had a really good relationship with is against gay marriage. I couldn't believe it—I never would have thought he was so intolerant. It's been a little uncomfortable for me since that conversation. I don't think he realizes it yet, but I have been avoiding him. I'm not sure that I can be friends with him anymore. How should I handle it?—Jervonte

A: Dear Jervonte,

I'm sorry, but it seems you are equally "intolerant" about someone else's viewpoint. Differences are what add spice to relationships. Differences inspire conversation, which is how we learn about the other side's point of view. Differences have always existed and always will.

However, if that is how you feel, then you have your answer.

Having a different point of view about this or any other subject hasn't changed him, only how you choose to see him.

Options:

- While I admire conviction, only you can decide what is right for you.
- Take the middle-school route; avoid and make excuses. (This only drags out the break-up process and makes for awkward conversation.)
- Speak to him privately, explaining your strong stance on this subject and see where it goes. (Hopefully, "respect" is extended from both sides.)

- Speak to him privately, explaining that you cannot be friends with anyone who is opposed to this topic (or any other that you don't see eye to eye on).

Vive la différence!

....

COWORKER
CAMARADERIE

It's easy and pretty common to develop a familiar relationship with a coworker when you're with them all day, every day—and just as easy to develop a hostile relationship.

Becoming "friends" outside of work is great . . . except when it turns ornery or proves to be an incompatible association.

Sometimes, when you hang out in social settings, you see actions or traits that are not so favorable. They may even bring work-related issues into the relationship.

What if they start to alienate themselves from you? How awkward is that when you have to see them every day. An after-work-hours relationship that has gone frosty can affect your job performance and your relationship with coworkers (e.g., gossip and taking sides).

Develop "friendships" slowly. Get to know each other through conversations. Discuss different topics and listen for comments and opinions. That can give you a clue about who they are. Either proceed or keep it professionally friendly.

She Be Trippin': Colloquial Vocab

From the Audience:

Q: I identify ethnically as Mexican. I work with an African American woman, "Jeannette." We've become friends and have started to go shopping and taking walks on the weekends. There have been a couple of times when I've used expressions that are popular and used predominantly by African Americans, such as, "Gurrrl," "Oh, no, he di'int," and "She be trippin'." I don't mean it to be degrading, and I am not aspiring to be somebody I'm not; I just love the terms. The other day, I used one of these terms, and she gave me a look. I've stopped saying them since then. Should I talk to her about it? —Esmeralda

A: Dear Esmeralda,

Does your friend Jeannette use those colloquial terms? Just askin'.

To answer your question, speak with her right away. Don't make it a big, dramatic scene. Ask her if it bothers her. You can explain your point of view and see where it goes. You may find that the "look" you thought she gave you wasn't even directed at you. Tactful, kind, respectful discussions can solve a lot of misunderstanding and suppositions. (This is a perfect example in favor of time-honored traditions and formalities.) If you find out that Jeannette is bothered by it (she should have told you), simply tell her you meant no harm, apologize, and stop it.

After that, if she becomes distant at work, you'll really

know how she felt. Or maybe what you perceived to be a blossoming friendship just wasn't. Keep it professional and cordial at work.

You can always fall back on "*pues mira,*" "*papi chulo,*" or "*oye chica.*" Who knows? She might find them amusing and start using them, too.

Finally, I think it's a compliment when someone adopts mannerisms, aspects, or traits of a friend or person they admire. If a term or word is used and delivered in a humorous, endearing, friendly, and innocent manner (you can usually tell), let it go, and accept it as such. Some people use this to build camaraderie. Whatever you think about this, reserve the slang for when you're off the clock.

....

THE STOCKROOM PLUNDERER

From the Audience:

Q: I walked into my coworker's cubicle the other day, obviously catching her off guard. She was loading a bunch of office supplies into a gym bag. Neither one of us said anything, so after a few awkward seconds, I walked away. I had to talk to someone, so I told a trusted coworker about it. He said he caught her doing the same thing a month ago. What should we do about this? —Armande

A: Dear Armande,

Obviously, it is not an isolated incident. If you know, and

your coworker knows, who knows how many others know as well.

Stealing will get you sacked, but not if no one finds out.

Ethically and morally, the honorable thing to do is to notify your supervisor first and then the HR department. You will no doubt be asked to make an official statement. Whether you can remain anonymous or not is up to your company's policy.

What are your other options? Here are a few to consider:

- Together with your coworker, privately speak to the office supply plunderer. Ask her to return the stolen goods. (She may deny it, refuse to return the items, or become angry and tell you to go . . . well, you know the rest.)

- Tell the plunderer that either she must report herself or you will. (She may promise to return the items and never ever do it again.) Listen to your gut on this one.

- Ignore the incident entirely. (If it is ever found that you knew about it and allowed it, your character will be implicated. Worth it?)

- Report it to your supervisor and let him or her handle it.

- Protecting someone else's character is commendable, but not if it is at the expense of damaging your own.

If we get right down to it, taking a pen, making copies of personal stuff, using a stamp on personal mail, making a personal long-distance call, taking a binder because your child needs it for his report, or taking sugar packs from the lunch room are all stealing.

> "Be more concerned with your character than your reputation, because your character is what you really are, while your reputation is merely what others think you are."—John R. Wooden, American basketball player and coach

By the way, self-justified stealing is still stealing: "I don't get paid enough." "There's tons of toilet paper rolls; they won't miss it." "They owe me. I don't get overtime." "The company can afford it." "It's just one." "I don't have time to go shopping."

YOUR COWORKER IS AN EX-CON?

> Did you know? This statistic has become so mainstream that a long-running children's program, *Sesame Street*, introduced a new character, a child whose dad is locked up.
>
> "It is all one to me if a man comes from Sing Sing Prison or Harvard. We hire a man, not his history."—Malcom S. Forbes, publisher of *Forbes Magazine*

Oh, you've never worked with an ex-con? You probably have, or will eventually. According to the Pew Research Center, there are 2.7 million minor children with a parent in jail or prison. [19] That means about one in every twenty-eight

American children have a parent who is incarcerated.

From the Audience:

I once let an ex-con use my phone. When he returned it he started asking me about my vacation. He had gone through my picture gallery! After that, I learned my lesson. Never let an ex-con borrow ANYTHING!

> Stereotyping is a spontaneous thing that typically stems from our experiences or upbringing—most of us aren't proud of it, but it happens from time to time and at varying degrees.

What Ex-Cons Would Like You to Consider:

Get to know me for who I am, not for my "record." I can't erase history, but it doesn't have to define the present.

You may be able to trust me only to a certain extent—I get it and accept it.

I see you trying to discreetly move your purse closer to you when you see me coming. That is an unimaginative and obvious move; please masquerade it as though you were putting it away or making room for me to sit—we'll both know what you're doing, but it isn't as discourteous.

I may come back with a humorous remark after you mouth off a prison joke or a who-done-it comment—this is not an invitation to keep 'em coming; it serves only to lessen the awkwardness or embarrassment of your comment.

I'm okay with not having the key to the front door or the supply cabinet. In fact, this guarantees that when something is missing, I won't have security waiting for me by my work-station when I come in to work.

I can't stop you from expressing curiosity about my previous "dark side," but please catch a clue when I use polite remarks to discourage you.

The United States Department of Justice states that approximately two-thirds of ex-offenders will likely be rearrested within three years of release. The Institute on Women and Criminal Justice states that the female state prison population growth has outpaced male growth in the past quarter century. What is the answer?

For starters, giving an ex-con a break and supporting successful programs that unlock the trauma and help us gain understanding into the addictions that often lead to criminal behavior. What if I were born to a family of drug addicts? What if my parents were in prison, and I was abandoned? What if I were abused and neglected as a child? What, then, might be my path?

There are stories of success . . . certainly proof that residency and recovery programs can work.

—San Francisco Bay Area Women's Residency Program Director

The Curious Coworker: So, tell me everything; what were some of the things you were into? Is prison really like that TV show? Did you do any of those things?

The Polite Ex-Con: When I say things like:

- Whatever you are thinking, I probably did it.
- I'll never tell.
- I understand your curiosity, but that was my old life.
- I prefer to disregard that part of my life.

- Let's just say that I learned a lot and it allowed me to be who I am today.
- My motto is that the past is in the past, and it should stay there.
- Thank you for being so interested, but I prefer not to revisit the past.
- I believe in keeping my personal life personal in the workplace.

It is my way of telling you that it isn't any of your business, or that I don't know you well enough to share that part of my life. There's a lot more to me than my time in prison. We could delve into an unpleasant time in your life, and I could ask you a lot of questions, but I wouldn't do that to you because I understand that it doesn't define you and it's none of my business.

An ex-con also understands that there are mean people in the world. A fundamentally mean or manipulative person will find something about anyone and everyone who they can take jab at. Ex-con, divorced, overweight, religious, not religious, recovering addict, passed over for a promotion, broken heart, from the South, etc. You get the point. We just need to know that people can change—and we need to be willing to let them.

....

YOUR COWORKER IS A RECOVERING ADDICT/ALCOHOLIC?

If you knew someone was in recovery from addiction, would you treat them differently? Sometimes, to ease our feeling of discomfort, to show open mindedness, to relate, or to show compassion, we begin to tell all about our dear Aunt Augusta who has a drinking problem. Do you really think that's what the recovering addict/alcoholic wants to hear or talk about? The answer is "no"—unless perhaps you are also on your way to an AA or NA meeting. Still, such conversations are certainly not appropriate in the workplace.

P.S. No need to pass along this newfound information. Keep it to yourself.

The Company Picnic, Holiday Party, or Dinner

If your coworker tells you that they aren't attending a company event because there will be alcohol served, don't even start trying to talk them into it. It's called boundaries and respect!

Please don't push it with well-intentioned remarks like:

- "I'll stand next to you in case you reach for a drink." (And do what? Knock it out of their hand? Um, no one will notice that.)

- "When I see the server approach, I'll give you a warning." (Oh, what fun! A drinky-sitter.)

- "Just don't drink." (Ahem, that's the whole point.)

By the way, it's not your place to spread the news about their absence or why.

Don't I Know You From . . . ?

From the Audience:

Q: I go to a couple of Narcotics Anonymous (NA) meetings, one near work and the other near home. The other day, I was having lunch with a few coworkers when "Cicero" walked up to our table trying to place me. Then, suddenly, he blurted, "Oh, yeah, haven't I seen you at the NA meeting on 41st Avenue?" I stumbled on my words and ended up admitting to attending NA meetings. Luckily, my coworkers were cool about it. In the future, how can I handle this?—Monica

A: Dear Monica,

I guess Cicero missed the whole "anonymous" idea? You could go to the "white lie" method of dealing with things, although white lies aren't always effective and are probably not encouraged by the "NA"-type programs.

Consider these options:

- "I'm sorry, but I don't know what you're talking about . . . have a good day." (It's a little abrupt, but hey, sometimes it's the only way out.)
- "I get that a lot . . . I seem to have one of those faces." (Then look away.)
- "No, I don't believe I've ever seen you." (If you can do it without being detected by the others, give Cicero a glare, and hope he gets it.)

- "Yes, we have met, but it wasn't there ... I'll probably remember later. Would you please excuse me, we're on our lunch break." (Smile and look away.)

Once the cat is out of the bag, your options are:

- "That was a long time ago, I can't believe he recognized me." (Take a bite of your salad, and hope no one probes.)
- "Well, now you know. Any questions?" (Be prepared to respond and decline to respond if the question is way too personal.)
- "I had a problem with narcotics/alcohol. I am fortunate to be in recovery." (I'll bet that at least one person in the group will bring up a friend or family member who has also struggled.)
- "I value my privacy. If you don't mind, I prefer not to discuss it, and ask for your confidentiality. Thank you." (Warning: word may spread anyway.)

By the way, the next time you see Cicero, I'd make a point of politely reminding him about what the second letter stands for.

Some people in recovery openly wear their "chips" or "pins." This doesn't mean that you point and ask them to explain each chip. If they talk about it, just listen and end the conversation with an optimistic tone or cheer. Use common sense, and don't invite them to have drinks after work or surprise them with a bottle of bourbon at the holiday gift exchange.

Drinks with the Coworkers

Dear well-intentioned coworkers,

I might not be able to explain why I don't participate in after-work functions. I may have an ankle bracelet that requires me to be home by a certain time. I may have to return home on time to prove to CPS (Child Protective Services) that I am fit so that I can regain custody of my children. I may not want to be around alcohol.

When someone declines a drink, don't ask them why; it isn't any of your business, and it is definitely unprofessional to pry. Their reason may be as simple as they've had one already today. They might be a recovering alcoholic. They might be the designated driver. They might be picking up their child. They might have a health issue or religious belief that forbids them from consuming alcohol. (If they say that they are Muslim, Mormon, or a member of any other religion that discourages drinking, and they don't fit the stereotype, accept it—they may be using levity to get you to stop bugging them or they may actually be practicing. You can't be the judge.) They might not like what is being offered. They might be one of those people who can fun without spirits, or they might not like alcohol at all. LEAVE THEM ALONE!

From the Audience:

Most of my coworkers are college-aged. I've told a few about my recovery ... I'm proud to show them that you can have fun without alcohol or drugs.—Courageous Woman in Recovery

Can We All Meet at Your Place?

From the Audience:

Q: I work at a great company. It's small, so everyone knows everyone. Lately, they've been taking turns meeting up at someone's house, and from there we all go out to dinner or a movie. Because I live kind of far away from everyone, no one has suggested meeting at my house until recently. How can I avoid this? I live in a safe house. I'm not ashamed of it, but I can't divulge the location. I can't put them off much longer. —Norma

A: Dear Norma,

This is a prickly dilemma. If you believe in "white lies," the problem is easily solved. You can use excuses like:

1. "Parking is awful."
2. "My roommate is asleep at that time."
3. "I refuse to have anyone over until I buy some furniture. You understand."
4. "I run into too many people I know in my neighborhood."
5. "My landlords live above me, so we'd have to be very quiet."
6. "My lease agreement doesn't allow me to have a lot of guests." (Except for the "lease" part, this is true.)
7. "I'm renting a room from a family, so I can't really have anyone over." (Some truth to it.)

However, if you are not comfortable telling white lies, you

can modify 5, 6, and 7; there is truth to all of them to explain your living situation without divulging the details.

....

WORKING WITH
KINFOLK
AND FRIENDS

If you and your best friend or aunt both work for a large company, and in different departments, what could possibly go wrong? Plenty. However, the chances of direct conflict or competition are slim. Nevertheless, misunderstandings and gossip knows no boundaries.

But what if you own your own business and you've hired your cousin, your best friend, and now your cousin's fiancé? Before it goes too far, ask yourself this common sense question: Would I have hired them if they had walked in off the street? If the answer is "no" (or even "probably not"), you are in trouble!

Sometimes family members' and friends' attitudes about working for a start-up or small company owned by a family member or friend is distorted. They might assume, "More perks!" Uh, sorry. In reality, it's usually a lot fewer perks. That needs to be made clear before they are hired. Even more importantly, they must be committed and formally agree to the arrangement.

This goes both ways. You, the boss might take liberties or make requests beyond the scope of the job description.

Expecting them to stay after work to help you with something, or come in over the weekend (without compensation) as "a friend."

Consider creating a "policies and procedures" manual. Be sure to include rules about time off, children at work, vacations, job descriptions, salary increases, and firing and quitting procedures. Hand it out to every employee with an "I understand and agree to" signature page. This will not only protect you, but will also provide your "employee" with a clear picture of your working relationship. In addition, it helps formalize the relationship.

There's nothing like a family squabble to ruin the next holiday gathering. Be clear. Be consistent. Try to limit personal life discussions to the break room or at the pub after work. And most of all, don't gossip behind anyone's back; go directly to the person and deal with it. When people have to pick sides, you know it's gotten out of hand.

....

MAN'S BEST FRIEND: DISTRACTION AND IDLENESS OR SERENITY AND PRODUCTIVITY?

Whether you own your own business or your company allows you to bring in your dog, please keep Mambo under control, especially when a coworker or client is present. There are some companies rethinking the whole "bring your

I've got Bandit on my mind (and my clothes).

dog to work" policy. They are finding that it is more distracting than beneficial.

Think about it. Your focus is regularly interrupted. Mambo did something cute; Mambo needs to visit the fire hydrant, again; Mambo needs a snack or a hug; Mambo barks every time someone walks by; etc. Not to mention the dog lovers in the building who pop in to pet Mambo—yet another interruption. When do you get your work done?

> I think dogs are great; I just don't want one. Boy, do I get grief for that.
> I do understand that a pet becomes a part of your life and family. And I am the first to admit that they are remarkable animals. They are service dogs, caring companions, and military dogs, as my friend and author, Maria Goodavage's penetrating book, *Soldier Dogs*, details.

From the Audience:

Q: I recently went on an interview and left with a runny nose and watering eyes. The HR Director had her dog in the office—I'm allergic. When she took me on a tour of the place, I noticed that a few other people also had their dogs with them. I was afraid to say anything because, as I said, I want the job and don't want to offend anyone and lose my chances of getting it. What are my options?—Dixie

A: Dear Dixie,

The solution is unfortunate, but simple: you can't take the job. You can't ask them to leave their pooch at home—well, you can, but I doubt that they'll change the pet policy just for you.

Options are few:

- Wear a face mask. (If you work in the back or in a little corner tucked away, that might be okay. But if you see clients, they might wonder what germs you're trying not to spread.)
- Suck on allergy tablets all day. (Please don't. It's addictive, makes you drowsy, and can sometimes upset your stomach . . . could you handle that every day?)
- Get an allergy shot (hoping it's for the right breed).
- Bring in a humidifier and/or an allergen purifier. (Maybe the company will provide one for you.)

I'm sorry, but this is a growing dilemma in the workplace. (Please hear me out before you throw the book down.)

Has the whole taking-Fifi-everywhere-I-go movement gone too far? Not if you are a pet lover.

Pet-lovers, please consider this:

- Some people are afraid of dogs. (By the way, please do not lecture them on why they shouldn't be! It's their fear, and you are not a therapist.)

- Some people have allergies and, therefore, cannot be around a dog.

- People wear clothes that they'd prefer to keep pet-hair and slobber-free.

- People may not want Mambo's enthusiastic greeting snagging their tights or scratching their leather boots.

- People may be in a hurry to discuss the issue at hand and do not wish to forcibly take time to greet Mambo (and possibly hurt your feelings with their lack of interest).

- You don't smell it, but your office might stink of dog—making it unpleasant for others.

- By the way, if your dog rips or snags your co-worker's tights, or chomps at their breakfast burrito, should you/would you reimburse them? Just askin'.

Are you barkin' mad yet? Are you howling out loud, "If someone doesn't like my dog, then they can *va' al diavolo!* (It sounds less hateful in Italian.) Well, I understand, and you can certainly feel that way, but you are in a work setting, working with *other* people. Imposing Mambo's affections on others is not professional, respectful, or considerate.

P.S. Taking pictures of Mambo during work hours and

Dear "pet parent": Not everyone feels the same sentiment about your beloved pooch, Mambo. Please don't get angry at the humans; it's just the way it is. Please don't assume that everyone relishes being jumped on, licked, rubbed, sniffed, forced to pet Mambo, forced to go on and on about how adorable he is, forced to hear about the adorable things he does . . . unless they also have a precious pooch by their side; then it's all good.

P.S. Keep a lint roller handy; your guests will appreciate it. You might also consider keeping a crate or "special spot" for Mambo to retreat to when you have office guests.

Dear "non-pet enthusiasts": Acknowledge the pooch. If you aren't in the middle of dining, a quick pat on the head is a nice gesture. A friendly comment about Mambo would be appreciated by the "pet parent." You may ask the "pet parent" to keep Mambo from jumping on you, or you can just take a step back. Please refrain from lecturing the "pet parent" about their technique or affection for Mambo."

posting on social media is just wrong (unless it's during your break time).

....

SUPERSTITIOUS

From the Audience:

Q: I don't know why, but I am a very superstitious person. In fact, I use a vacation day so that I'm off on Friday the Thirteenths. When I voice or display the superstition, I either get the evil eye or austere sighs from my coworkers. One woman sharply told me to stop it and to leave her alone. I don't want to make enemies; I do it out of concern for them. What should I do? —Gloria

What else could go wrong?

A: Dear Gloria,

I can't tell you to just stop it because that would be imposing my disbelief on something you obviously believe to be true. With that said, your professional reputation might already have a little smudge. If your rituals interfere with your job, disturb your coworkers' duties, or invade their privacy, that is a problem.

For example, if your coworker spills salt, it is not appropriate for you to reach over and undue the curse. Similarly, it is not appropriate for you to force your colleague to rub your lucky rabbit's foot before he gives a presentation.

In fact, your actions could be equated to someone proselytizing about religion or lifestyles choices, or selling timeshares while on the company's time.

Having a "lucky number" or "jumping over cracks" so that you don't break your mother's back can be fun, but not if it interferes with or affects your job.

You are free to believe whatever you want, but please don't let your beliefs or superstitions interfere with a professional work environment. This same advice applies to someone who is vociferously religious or political. Feel free to practice your beliefs on your own time.

> Did you know? Primitive man believed that salt was a magical substance that could be used for both good and evil. Salt protected them from the devil when it was realized that it could also preserve food; more than likely, it could preserve people. Spilled salt: Since common belief was that good spirits lived on the right side and evil ones on the left, people threw salt over the left shoulder right into the eyes of the Devil. [20]

DO YOU SPEAK-AH MY LANGUAGE?

From the Audience:

Q: At work, some of my coworkers who speak Chinese always greet me in "our" language. I feel uncomfortable, especially when there is someone else in the office or lunch room. I reply in English, but they continue speaking in Chinese. They have lectured me about being ashamed of my heritage. I'm not ashamed. I was taught to speak English in the workplace. How do I explain myself to them without further insulting them?—Meili

A: Dear Meili,

I applaud your decision to be considerate of others and

take a professional stand, especially in the workplace.

You are correct in your decision to speak English in the workplace. An occasional, brief exchange in Chinese, when non-Chinese coworkers aren't present, is fine and understandable.

Like you, I was taught to speak English outside the home, a different language (Spanish) inside the home. However, if you're on a picnic, at a restaurant, or in a non-work environment, go for it.

If you prefer to sit with only same-heritage coworkers, here are some things to consider:

Sitting in a circle of "your own kind" alienates others. Most people are not going to approach a table where a foreign language is being spoken. I'd be wondering if you'd stop when I sat down. Would you be peeved because I showed up? Would you get up and walk away? I would rather avoid finding out, so I'd choose to sit elsewhere.

Sitting in a circle of "your own kind" gives the impression of restrictiveness or exclusivity. What I mean is, if a manager sees that you sit with only "your own kind," he or she may perceive that you are not comfortable outside your group or unwilling or uninterested in integrating to build a cohesive and connected work atmosphere.

Sitting in a circle of "your own kind" can prohibit you from getting to know other coworkers. Building relationships within the company is a good way to network, learn of opportunities, establish rapport with different departments, and develop a list of go-to coworkers.

Sitting in a circle of "your own kind" prohibits other

people from getting to know you. (You don't want them missing out on that, do you?)

Meili, there are a few options on how to handle this situation:

- Greet them in Chinese and proceed in English, no matter what. (Hope that they eventually get it.)
- Sit with them and chat in Chinese for a few minutes to make them hush, then excuse yourself. (However, if you are seen at the table by a coworker/boss, you will be lumped in.)
- Privately speak to the one or two who badger you, and explain your stance or reason as to why you are an English-speaker in the workplace. (This may or may not have an effect, but at least they'll leave you alone.)
- Check with HR for guidance.
- Change your lunch time. (Avoidance is an option; sometimes it's the simplest way to go.)

Counterpoint: It's my break time; I can do and say whatever I want. Don't listen if you don't wanna hear it!

Response: Yes, you can do or say whatever you want. However, while you are on company property, you want to be seen as a professional, don't you? Do your actions show you in the best light? Do they affect your coworkers? Is it necessary for you to do or say those things right now?

Wrap up: This professional code of conduct is not limited to the Chinese language. This can be applied to other languages, female-only groups, ethnically based groups, or any other exclusive group makeup.

Don't limit whom you get to know in the workplace. Whomever you hang with or whatever you do outside the workplace is your business.

....

PREGNANCY PROBLEMS

Don't Touch the Tummy!

He loves it when I s-i-n-g to him.

From the Audience:

Q: I am six months pregnant, but I feel like a lucky charm when people walk by and give my bulging tummy a rub. How do I delicately tell them, "Hands off!"? —Pamela

A: Dear Pamela,

This is a touchy subject (giggle, giggle). You might agree that most people who touch the belly do so because it stirs up warm and fuzzy feelings inside their heart. However, that does not give them permission to invade your space. Here are a few comebacks to help you cope. You could try saying:

- "You know, my tummy/skin has become quite sensitive lately."
- "Gosh, I have this superstition about having people touch my belly." (A white lie—this could backfire if the belly rubber asks about the superstition.)
- "Thanks for caring, but I'm a little skittish/protective with my belly right now . . . I guess it's the "mother" in me coming through."

By the way, Pamela, I presume that you don't work in a corporate environment where touching someone, especially of the opposite sex, is practically prohibited.

Lactation Breaks . . . Again!

Seeing the rolling eyes, hearing the heavy sighs and snide remarks as the pumping mommy walks by, yet another time—this, accompanied by guilt, is what some breast-pumping mothers experience in the workplace.

Most people agree that providing a baby with mom's milk is a commendable and health-minded decision. But, it seems that we draw the line when it affects "me."

There are laws in place that require companies (terms vary) to provide a specific room where the new mother cannot be interrupted. For how long? Up to one year.

I don't want to get into the details of the law. I do want to address the coworkers' attitudes toward the pumping parent.

Coworkers' perspective: Just as with the smoker, who requires additional breaks, you, the pumping parent may experience a snide remark or a scornful look—especially if I, your coworker, have to pick up your workload, take messages, deal with frustrated callers or office guests, or repeatedly explain that you are away from your desk yet again.

I might be full of understanding and willing to assist for one month, maybe two, but for one year?! Would you be willing to cover for someone for that long? Should I, along with your other coworkers, be forced to cover for you, the pumping parent? That, I believe, is a question for the Human Resources department.

Pumping parent's perspective: Well, I do have the law on my side; that pretty much settles that. However, laws can't dictate people's reactions to the laws.

What can the pumping parent do to settle down the overworked and resentful coworkers?

- Say, "Thank you" every day and after every additional or lengthy break.

- Find out your overworked coworkers' favorite beverage or pastry, and bring it in for them every week.

- If they've gone above and beyond that week, have flowers delivered or buy them something they enjoy—a book, a candle, a gift card, etc.

- If there are several coworkers within your department, you might consider buying them lunch every couple of weeks or bringing in specialty coffee.

- Offer them your time. Cover their phones during the lunch hour, allowing them to go out as a group. Assist them with their project. Offer to make copies when you make yours. Your time and assistance is probably the most relevant and significant way to show your gratitude. I'm sure you can think of other ways to express your gratitude.

Lastly, remember that they are doing you a favor. Even when they don't do it with a smile on their face, they are covering for you.

More Pregnancy Pointers

- Be careful about guessing the baby's gender. (Some parents either want to wait until the birth to know or keep it to themselves until they are ready to divulge it to ~~you~~ the world.)
- Avoid telling the larger-sized mom that she must be having twins. (Wow, did you stick your foot in your mouth!)
- Don't insist that it is a boy or girl because you are clairvoyant, the baby is sitting high, the baby is sitting low, etc. (A friendly guess is fine, but then stop it!)
- Avoid stating what their preference must be since they already have a boy/girl.

- Never point out unattractive or sensitive side effects of pregnancy like acne, bloating, frizzy hair, weight gain, eating habits, waddling, etc. (Oh, I guess you never have a bad hair day.)

- Don't lecture pregnant women on what not to eat, how much to eat, or any other pointers. (If you have something to share, do so without a superior tone. And if they don't seem interested, stop it.)

- Don't give them your list of baby names. And please don't negatively comment on *their* list of baby names.

- Please don't share your pregnancy horror stories—especially with a first-time mom. (Why would you do that?)

- If the mother is not married, don't ask who the father is.

- If the mother is gay, don't ask who the father is.

- Never ask about the circumstances of conception. (That's none of your business.)

- Don't ask whether they want more babies. (Again, it's none of your business!)

> Please don't ask any women you see with a belly, "When are you due?" #toorisky

Fashions and trendy phrases come and go, as do formalities—but courtesy, consideration of others, respect, tact, humility and humor should never go out of style, even in this fast-paced, disconnected world.

I hope I've succeeded in making "etiquette" a little less intimidating and a lot more modern and practical.

Thank you. May you be successful in your pursuits.

KEY POINTS:

- Leery about working with an ex-con? Remember, HR apparently decided they were competent. Who are you to judge?
- Respect a person's answer; don't insist.
- Set policies and procedures before hiring family or friends.
- Falling in love at the office can happen and succeed; just don't get all high school about it.
- Is having Fido at work helping or hindering your productivity? Rethink: career or kennel.
- Cliques at work don't work.
- Respect your coworkers' body and space.
- The workplace lunch room is not just like your family dinner table.
- Sometimes you don't need to comment. Just let it go.

> "You can easily judge the character of a man by how he treats those who can do nothing for him." –Johan Wolfgang von Goethe, German writer (1749-1832)

Etiquette is an attitude.

SOURCES

1. Panati, Charles. *Extraordinary Origins of Everyday Things*. New York: Harper & Row, 1990.

2. Ibid.

3. Potter, Carole. *Knock on Wood & Other Superstitions*. New York: Bonanza Books, 1983. 231.

4. Web MD. "Gas, Bloating, and Burping—Topic Overview," *WebMD*, 2011. http://www.webmd.com/heartburn-gerd/tc/gas-bloating-and-burping-topic-overview.

5. Fernandez, Colin. "Better in than Out: African Country Set to Make Breaking Wind a Crime," *DailyMail*, 2011. http://www.dailymail.co.uk/news/article-1351174/African-country-set-make-breaking-wind-crime.html

6. Panati. Charles. *Extraordinary Origins of Everyday Things*. New York: Harper & Row, 1990. 199.

7. Pearson, Christine and Christine Porath. *The Cost of Bad Behavior: How Incivility is Damaging to Your Business and What to Do About It*, New York: Penguin Group. 2009.

8. Whitmore, Jacqueline. *Business Class: Etiquette Essentials for Success at Work*, New York: St. Martin's Press. 2005.

9. Merriam-Webster Dictionary

10. Douglas B. Smth, *Ever Wonder Why?*, Fawcett: New York: 1991. 1

11. Margaret Visser, *The Ritual of Dinner—The Origins, Evolution, Eccentricities, and Mean of Table Manners*, Penguin Group, New York: 1991, 163.

12. Potter, Carole. *Knock on Wood & Other Superstitions*. New York: Bonanza Books, 1983. 163.

13. "Carrying More Than You Bargained For?" *Initial: The Experts in Hygiene*, 2012. http://www.initial.co.uk/news/2012/handbag-hygiene.html

14. Holt, Emily. *Encyclopaedia of Etiquette, A book of Manners for Everyday Use*. Doubleday Page & Co.: New York. 1921. 400.

15. Holt, Emily. *Encyclopaedia of Etiquette, A book of Manners for Everyday Use*. Doubleday Page & Co.: New York. 1921. 156.

16. Axtell, Roger E. *Gestures: The Do's and TABOOs of Body Language Around the World*, John Wiley & Sons, Inc.: New York. 1991. 82.

17. Evins, Karlen. *I Didn't Know That*, Scribner: New York. 2007. 4.

18. Potter, Carole. *Knock on Wood & Other Superstitions*. New York: Bonanza Books, 1983. 100.

19. The Economic Mobility Project and the Public Safety Perfomance Project of the Pew Charitable Trusts. http://www.pewtrusts.org/uploadedFiles/wwwpewtrustsorg/Reports/Economic_Mobility/Collateral%20Costs%20FINAL.pdf?n=5996

20. Potter, Carole. *Knock on Wood & Other Superstitions*. New York: Bonanza Books, 1983. 168–169.

ABOUT THE AUTHOR

Rosalinda Randall is a modern-day pundit on tact and civility. While she wasn't brought up in a finger-bowl type of home, she was surrounded by more important things like respect, kindness, boundaries, consistency, consequences, tons of love, values, and a healthy dose of humor. By lending personality and some humor of her own to the age-old and sometimes boring topic of etiquette, Rosalinda has been successfully improving workplace environments and relationships with enthusiastic and insightful advice for more than fourteen years.

Rosalinda's tips have been featured in *Forbes*, *Woman's Day*, YahooShine, Small Biz Technology, *MetroWest Daily News*, *Winter Bride 2013*, *Ser Padres*, and other publications.

One of her favorite missions is serving as a consultant to formerly incarcerated women, many of whom are now very dear to her heart.

Originally born and raised in Southern California, she now lives in Northern California with her husband, Christopher.

For more information about her company and services, please visit her website: www.yourrelationshipedge.com.

ABOUT FAMILIUS

Visit Our Website: www.familius.com

Our website is a different kind of place. Get inspired, read articles, discover books, watch videos, connect with our family experts, download books and apps and audiobooks, and along the way, discover how values and happy family life go together.

Join Our Family

There are lots of ways to connect with us! Subscribe to our newsletters at www.familius.com to receive uplifting daily inspiration, essays from our Pater Familius, a free ebook every month, and the first word on special discounts and Familius news.

Become an Expert

Familius authors and other established writers interested in helping families be happy are invited to join our family and contribute online content. If you have something important to say on the family, join our expert community by applying at:

www.familius.com/apply-to-become-a-familius-expert

Get Bulk Discounts

If you feel a few friends and family might benefit from what you've read, let us know and we'll be happy to provide you with quantity discounts. Simply email us at specialorders@familius.com.

Facebook: www.facebook.com/paterfamilius

Twitter: @familiustalk, @paterfamilius1